New Age
HYPNOSIS

DR. BRUCE GOLDBERG

1998
Llewellyn Publications
St. Paul, Minnesota 55164-0383, U.S.A.

FIRST EDITION
Second Printing, 1998

Cover design by Lisa Novak
Cover photo from Digital Stock
Editing and interior design by Connie Hill

Library of Congress Cataloging-in-Publication Data
Goldberg, Bruce, 1948–
    New age hypnosis / by Bruce Goldberg
        p. cm. --
    Includes bibliographical references and index.
    ISBN 1–56718–320–4 (pbk.)
        1. Hypnotism.   2. Autogenic training.   3. New Age movement.
I. Title.
BF1152.G65   1998
131—dc21   97–38817
                                                                CIP

Llewellyn Publications
A Division of Llewellyn Worldwide, Ltd.
St. Paul, Minnesota 55164-0383, U.S.A.

HYPNOSIS AS A SOULFUL PROCESS

Believe it or not, you spend seven hours of every twenty-four-hour day in a state of natural hypnosis. You enter this state just before going to sleep and upon rising, as well as in daydreams, meditation, and yoga. Hypnosis is a natural and efficient waking state of the mind in which you are in communication with your higher self, offering you a tremendous opportunity for spiritual growth.

Now you can learn to maximize this state with the most comprehensive self-hypnosis program available. Besides the commonly known uses for hypnosis such as quitting smoking or losing weight, you can use hypnosis to further the evolution of your soul.

Dr. Goldberg has provided the scripts you need to guide you to your superconscious mind, or higher self. This will enable you to:

- Receive spiritual guidance from your higher self or Masters and Guides
- Scan past lives, the future of your current lifetime, and future lifetimes
- Contact departed loved ones
- Remove attached entities
- Protect yourself from the negativity of others
- Contact the souls of unborn children

What's more, you will discover additional benefits including:

- Elimination of tension and increased self-confidence
- Better concentration and improved memory
- Improved reflexes and heightened psychic awareness
- Increased self-confidence
- Pain control, and elimination of headaches, including migraines
- Strengthening of your immune system to resist disease
- Improved quality of people and circumstances you attract into your life
- Elimination of obsessive-compulsive behavior
- Improved personal relationships

Whatever you wish to change in your life, you can, with *New Age Hypnosis!*

ABOUT THE AUTHOR

Dr. Bruce Goldberg holds a B.A. degree in Biology and Chemistry, is a Doctor of Dental Surgery, and has an M.S. degree in Counseling Psychology. He retired from dentistry in 1989, and has concentrated on his hypnotherapy practice in Los Angeles. Dr. Goldberg was trained by the American Society of Clinical Hypnosis in the techniques and clinical applications of hypnosis.

Dr. Goldberg has been interviewed on the Donahue, Oprah, Leeza, Joan Rivers, The Other Side, Regis and Kathie Lee, Tom Snyder, Jerry Springer, Jenny Jones, and Montel Williams shows; by CNN, CBS News, and many others.

Through lectures, television and radio appearances, and newspaper articles, including interviews in *TIME, The Los Angeles Times,* and *The Washington Post,* Dr. Goldberg has conducted more than 33,000 past life regressions and future life progressions since 1974, helping thousands of patients empower themselves through these techniques. His cassette tapes teach people self-hypnosis, and guide them into past and future lives. He gives lectures and seminars on hypnosis, regression and progression therapy, and conscious dying; he is a also a consultant to corporations, attorneys, and local and network media. His first edition of *The Search for Grace* was made into a television movie by CBS. His third book, the award-winning *Soul Healing,* is a classic on alternative medicine and psychic empowerment. Dr. Goldberg's column "Hypnotic Highways" appears in *FATE* magazine.

Dr. Goldberg distributes cassette tapes to teach people self-hypnosis and to guide them into past and future lives. For information on self-hypnosis tapes, speaking engagements, or private sessions, Dr. Goldberg can be contacted directly by writing to:

Bruce Goldberg, D.D.S., M.S.
4300 Natoma Avenue
Woodland Hills, CA 91364
Telephone: (800) KARMA-4-U or (800) 527-6248
Fax: (818) 704-9189
email: karma4u@webtv.net
Web Site: drbrucegoldberg.idsite.com

Please include a self-addressed, stamped envelope with your letter.

ACKNOWLEDGMENTS

I would like to express my appreciation to Nancy J. Mostad, acquisitions and development manager for Llewellyn Publications, without whose interest in my work this relationship with Llewellyn would not exist. Words cannot express my gratitude to Carl Llewellyn Weschcke, president of Llewellyn Publications, for his encouragement and his interest in alternative medicine. He is most definitely a builder of bridges.

This book's final form would not be what it is without the assistance of my editor, Connie Hill. Thank you, Connie, for your kindness, professionalism, and helpful suggestions. I would also like to thank my patients for their participation and success at *New Age Hypnosis* techniques. Without their demonstration of the benefits of these metaphysical, yet natural, techniques, this book would not have been possible.

OTHER BOOKS BY DR. BRUCE GOLDBERG

Past Lives—Future Lives
The Search for Grace: The True Story of Murder
  and Reincarnation
Soul Healing
Peaceful Transition: The Art of Conscious Dying
  & the Liberation of the Soul
Look Younger, Live Longer: Add 25 to 50 Years to
  Your Life, Naturally

Forthcoming

Protected by the Light: The Complete Book of
  Psychic Self-Defense
Time Travelers from Our Future
Astral Voyages: Mastering the Art of Soul Travel
Dream Your Problems Away: Techniques for
  Dream Empowerment
The Ultimate Truth: The Light at the End of the Tunnel
Lose Weight Permanently & Naturally
The Future is Now: Custom Design Your Own Destiny
Spiritual Ascension: The Path to God

CONTENTS

NOTE TO THE READER

This book is the result of the professional experiences accumulated by the author since 1974, working individually with over 11,000 patients. The material included here is intended to complement, not replace, the advice of your own physician, psychotherapist, or other health care professional, whom you should always consult about your circumstances prior to starting or stopping any medication or any other course of treatment, exercise regimen, or diet.

At times, the masculine pronoun has been used as a convention. It is intended to imply both male and female genders where this is applicable.

Some of the minor details in the case histories have been altered to protect the privacy of the author's patients. All of the names used, except those of the celebrities mentioned, have been altered. Everything else in these pages is true.

INTRODUCTION

This workbook has three objectives. My main goal is to present a thorough discussion of hypnosis and its application to New Age disciplines such as reincarnation, karma, astral travel, and others. My second purpose is to teach you how to place yourself into a hypnotic trance and experience various metaphysical approaches from past life regression and future life progression to superconscious mind taps, out-of-body experiences, and soul plane ascension techniques. Finally, I will instruct you how to become a New Age hypnotherapist, if that is your goal.

Before you begin reading this book, please keep in mind a general principle of the universe. There are no absolute truths, including what I just said. It is not my purpose to present dogma; your truths are quite different than mine. I am merely attempting to impart my experience and knowledge gained from conducting more than 33,000 past life regressions and future life progressions since 1974, on more than 11,000 individual patients.

The techniques I developed in those many years are streamlined and simplified here so that anyone can apply them. Indeed, I teach my patients self-hypnosis with these same approaches. When you finish reading this book, you will have a better understanding of hypnosis, its characteristics, its stages, and its application to New Age experiences. You will also be able to induce a hypnotic trance, deepen it, maximize a clinically beneficial state, and return to the normal waking state a more spiritually evolved soul.

I have observed that people who buy books on hypnosis want primarily to learn techniques. With this in mind, I have included word-for-word scripts of many of the techniques I use in my Los Angeles office.

I have attempted to eliminate the padding and irrelevant material often found in books on hypnosis, while at the same time preserving the information and techniques that will quickly train anyone in this simple art. I have also included several case histories to illustrate these techniques.

As a scientist and clinician, I present this material from the perspective of an ethical practitioner. There are no "stage hypnotist" approaches—my very own heart and soul went into preparing this manuscript. I "practice what I preach," as I have used each and every technique on myself before working with others.

Hypnosis is a natural state of mind to everyone. All about us, in everyday life, the principles of hypnotism are evident, although for the most part unnoticed. Our very surroundings, conversations, and activities constantly offer hypnotic suggestion. "Highway hypnosis" and other daydream experiences occur spontaneously. Daily sustained and repeated advertising on radio and television subjects the listeners to many forms of hypnotic suggestions that usually are acted upon with no conscious realization by the listener.

Hypnosis is employed in our churches, schools, even in political speeches, with the aim of influencing our behavior. A knowledge of hypnosis and self-hypnosis and how to use the techniques is important for the layperson as well as the health professional. When you add New Age approaches to the list of ways to improve your life, you can easily see the purpose of this book.

There are many examples of New Age phenomena that one can experience and use to grow spiritually, whether it be an out-of-body experience, an angel encounter, or other metaphysical techniques. Hypnosis is the most efficient system I have experienced that can maximize these phenomena for one's own spiritual growth.

Even if you don't desire actual, practical applications of the extensive induction procedures found in this book, you will enjoy reading it, and you will derive great personal assurance from the knowledge you gain from this instructive and comprehensive work.

1

HYPNOSIS: WHAT IS IT?

Think of yourself driving on a routine trip, one that you have made hundreds of times, on a local highway. You pass by the same exits every day and often don't remember seeing the signs. Your eyes are open, and you can respond to someone beeping their horn or trying to pass you. You are daydreaming.

This form of daydreaming, studied by police departments and motor vehicle bureaus, is called "highway hypnosis" (freeway hypnosis if you live in California or Texas). It is a perfectly safe and natural state of mind.

All forms of daydreaming are natural levels of hypnosis. They are characterized by focused concentration, relaxation, lack of movement, and an increase in sensory reception. Other examples of natural day-to-day hypnosis are reading a book, watching television, doing detailed work for extended periods of time, and performing any enjoyable task where time appears to pass quickly.

We experience approximately four hours of daydreams or natural hypnotic states during our waking day. Our nighttime dreams are another form of hypnosis usually occurring during the REM (rapid eye movement) cycle of sleep. We dream for approximately three hours every night.

Projecting this out, we experience seven hours of natural hypnosis during every twenty-four-hour day cycle—approximately 2,500 hours in a year! A forty-year-old reader of this book would have spent an average of 100,000 hours in natural hypnosis throughout his or her life. That is equivalent to doing for eight uninterrupted hours a day, five days a week, fifty weeks per year for fifty years, some menial task that you have completed hundreds of times. Remember, this hypothetical reader is only forty years old!

Hypnosis is induced in our daily lives by repetitive commercials, a good orator, advertising propaganda, and evangelistic appeals. We set aside our *conscious mind proper* (beta brain wave level on the electroencephalograph) and establish direct communication with our *subconscious mind* (alpha brain wave).

There are two other brain waves, theta and delta, that represent light and deep sleep respectively, but they do not concern us in our discussion of hypnosis. Modern medicine has established the fact that hypnosis is not a sleep state. Early in the nineteenth century English physician James Braid coined the term "hypnosis," based on the Greek word *hypnos,* which means "sleep." Later Braid recognized his error and tried unsuccessfully to change the name of this discipline. In 1845 Braid wrote:

> The most startling proof that hypnotism is different from common sleep is the extraordinary effects produced by it....In passing into common sleep, the limbs become flaccid from cessation of muscular tone and action....In hypnotism the limbs are maintained in a state of tonic rigidity for any length of time I have thought to try, etc. In passing into

natural sleep anything held in the hand is soon allowed to drop from the grasp, but, in the 'artificial sleep' now referred to, it will be held more firmly than before falling asleep.[1]

Since a medium-level hypnotic trance is characterized by amnesia and deep levels of relaxation, it is not difficult to see how the layperson could make this erroneous association. Remember that the idea of hypnosis being a sleep state was implanted by stage hypnotists, novelists, and Hollywood.

The conscious mind proper is our ego. Easily distracted, the conscious mind's concentration rate is only twenty-five percent efficient. This state of mind analyzes and criticizes everything, and dies when the physical body dies. We spend about twelve hours a day in our conscious mind-proper state.

The subconscious or alpha state is most important to our understanding of hypnosis. Its concentration efficiency is nearly perfect at a minimum of ninety-five percent. We enter this state just before going to sleep and upon arising, as well as in periods of daydreaming, meditation, yoga, and similar mind states. As you can see, hypnosis (alpha) is not a sleep state, but a *natural* and efficient waking state of mind.

The characteristics of hypnosis are:

- It is a relaxed state.

- Concentration is focused.

- The body is (usually) immobile.

- We are hyperaware of our five senses.

- Rapid eye movements occur.

Many people assume that the hypnotist has control over the subject, again a misunderstanding based on pop culture's portrayal of hypnosis. The stage hypnotist bases his or her act on making you think that he or she controls the subject by suggesting

---

1 James Braid, *Neurypnology*, edited by A. E. Waite (London: George Redway, 1899).

embarrassing situations that are dutifully carried out by the volunteer on stage.

There is no control by the hypnotist. The subject's moral and ethical code can never be violated by suggestion alone. The reason the stage hypnotist is so successful is that he or she carefully selects very deep-level subjects who are extroverts and require that form of attention. I will discuss the depth of hypnotic trances in detail in chapter 4.

The best hypnotic subjects are people who have excellent memories, can express emotions easily, don't lose their train of thought easily, are not overly critical, are intelligent, and who can visualize easily. Children between the ages of eight and sixteen make the best subjects, but I will work with children as young as five.

Overly critical people who cannot visualize, have low levels of intelligence, are too logical, are inhibited, and have short attention spans make the poorest hypnotic subjects.

Hypnosis is simply a way of relaxing and setting aside the conscious mind proper, while at the same time activating the subconscious mind so that suggestions can be made directly, enabling the subject to act on these suggestions with greater ease and efficiency.

Hypnosis can be described by the following formula:

Misdirected attention + belief + expectation = hypnosis

The term "heterohypnosis" is used to describe the induction of a subject into a hypnotic trance by another person (the hypnotist). If one does this to him- or herself, we refer to this as self-hypnosis or autohypnosis.

Most hypnosis is self-hypnosis. The hypnotist does not project hypnosis onto the subject. The subject decides when to accept this hypnotic state. The "gift" of hypnosis always lies with the subject, not the hypnotist. The hypnotist may set the stage and create an appropriate environment, but he or she cannot force the hypnotic state on the subject.

Our subconscious mind is like a computer that stores everything we observe by our five senses. This also includes past and future life data, since the subconscious (soul) reincarnates and can never be destroyed. Many of us have been misprogrammed to feel that hypnosis is either dangerous or a form of mind control.

Fears and fallacies about hypnosis are commonly reported by my patients. Here is how I respond to these concerns:

- **The fallacy of mind control.** I have already pointed out that it is the subject, not the hypnotist, that determines whether the hypnotic state is to occur.

- **The fear of revealing secrets in trance.** The subject always maintains this control. If I ask a subject to answer a question about their past or future life experience, they can answer or not answer my query at their discretion. The hypnotist cannot force the subject to answer.

- **The fear of not remembering suggestions after the trance ends.** Only very deep level subjects will experience this type of amnesia. The hypnotist can eliminate this problem by giving an appropriate suggestion for the subject to remember everything when the trance ends.

- **The fallacy of symptom substitution.** In chapter 2, I discuss the superconscious mind tap and how it eliminates the true cause of this problem. Symptom substitution will not occur as long as the cause of an issue is removed.

- **The fear of not being able to leave the hypnotized state.** Hypnosis is a natural state of mind. We all come out of this state when we are ready. All of my scripts include wakening instructions.

- **The fear of being trapped in a past or future life.** I have conducted more than 33,000 past life regressions and future life progressions on more than 11,000 individual patients since 1974, and I have never had this problem.

There are no cases of this occuring reported in scientific literature either.

The list of benefits that can be attained through hypnotherapy covers every facet of life. Through hypnotherapy you can:

1. Increase relaxation and eliminate tension.

2. Increase and focus concentration.

3. Improve memory ("hypernesia").

4. Improve reflexes.

5. Increase self-confidence.

6. Control pain.

7. Improve sex life.

8. Increase organization and efficiency.

9. Increase motivation.

10. Improve interpersonal relationships.

11. Slow the aging process.

12. Facilitate a better career path.

13. Eliminate anxiety and depression.

14. Overcome bereavement.

15. Eliminate headaches, including migraine headaches.

16. Eliminate allergies and skin disorders.

17. Strengthen your immune system to resist any disease.

18. Eliminate habits, phobias, and other negative tendencies (self-defeating sequences).

19. Improve decisiveness.

20. Improve the quality of people, and circumstances in general, that you attract into your life.

21. Increase your ability to earn and hold onto money.

22. Overcome obsessive-compulsive behavior.

23. Improve the overall quality of your life.

24. Improve psychic awareness—ESP, meditation, astral projection (out-of-body experience), telepathy, superconscious mind taps, etc.

25. Eliminate the fear of death by viewing your past and future lives.

26. Attract a soul mate into your life.

27. Establish and maintain harmony of body, mind, and spirit.

SELF-IMPROVEMENT BY HYPNOSIS

Hypnosis is a subject of rich interest to nearly everyone. The fascination that it holds is its promise to open up a world of rich treasures and self-improvement as if by magic. Nearly all humans feel at sometime the desire or need to improve themselves. Genuine, legitimate improvements in one's self are never easy. They require persistence and determination to accomplish. Hypnosis seems to be the answer. After all, doesn't the hypnotist have the power to make people do things?

Actually, the hypnotist has no power, just skill. Skilled hypnotists in the past were professional entertainers. They deliberately tried to give the false impression that they had a "remarkable power" over the subject and could force him or her to do things. The power behind hypnosis lies with the subject and his or her mind. Charged and unleashed, he or she is free to release all their mental creative powers and bring them to bear with amazing results. The capacity of the human mind to solve and create is amazing and remarkable. Self-hypnosis and hypnotic techniques are ways to successfully reach and put to use more of one's own mind.

Your conscious mind is relatively weak. It vacillates continuously, and it will create an endless round of excuses as to why you should not bother with getting something done. It lacks the kind of stabilizing force that the subconscious possesses.

The subconscious mind can best be influenced when we are in a passive or relaxed state, such as in hypnosis. Hypnosis is pleasant. It is a state of deep concentration. This restful quieting of the mind cleanses it, opening it to pure and more elevated thoughts. Hypnosis builds both mental vigor and enthusiasm because it removes all the negative fears and thoughts that act as roadblocks to energy, inspiration, and accomplishment. You want to turn your wishes, ideas, or hopes into reality, or they remain meaningless to you. The subconscious is the best place to start the undertaking.

I suggest, therefore, that you set aside two ten-minute periods each day for the purpose of training your subconscious mind. The best time is very early in the morning, shortly after awakening. The second period can be at your convenience during the day—except just before bedtime, unless you are having difficulty in falling asleep.

A SELF-HYPNOSIS EXERCISE

The following is an exercise for self-hypnosis that I developed in my early years in private practice. You may find it useful to listen to a tape recording of yourself reading this script.

Stage 1

Go into a room and close the door to shut out distracting sounds. Lie down on a bed or couch and relax as best you can for from two to five minutes. The mind and body both will tend to relax as you lay inert, and this passive state will open a door into the subconscious mind. As you lie quietly, close your eyes and think of a warm, relaxing feeling.

Focus all your attention on the muscles in the toes of both of your feet. Imagine this warm, relaxing feeling spreading and surrounding the muscles of the toes of both feet, moving to the backs of both feet and to the heels and ankles. Now imagine this warm feeling moving up through the calf muscles of both legs to the kneecap and into the thigh muscles, meeting at the hip bone.

The warm, relaxing feeling is moving up the backbone to the middle of the back, surrounding the shoulder blades and moving into the back of the neck.

The warm, relaxing feeling is now moving into the fingers of both hands, just like it did with the toes. This feeling now spreads into the backs of both hands, palms, wrists, forearms, elbows, shoulders, and neck, relaxing each and every muscle along its path.

The warm, relaxing feeling now moves into the intestines, stomach, chest, and neck muscles.

This warm, relaxing feeling moves into the back of the head, scalp, and all the way to the forehead. Now, the facial muscles are relaxed; now the eyes (which are closed), bridge of the nose, jaws (the teeth are separated), chin, ear lobes, and neck. Now each and every muscle in the entire body is so completely relaxed.

When you actually develop a generalized, relaxed feeling throughout your body or a heaviness in your arms or legs, you have reached the light stages of hypnosis. Continue with the exercise for several days, then progress to the second stage, which is more advanced. The instructions are a mental dialogue that you will have with yourself. Read it over two or three times and absorb the general idea rather than trying to remember it word for word, or as an alternative, tape record yourself reading it aloud.

Stage 2

To go deeper into hypnosis is just about everybody's chief concern. This can be accomplished in a number of ways. One of the more common is to imagine a very pleasant and soothing scene, such as a green valley that you are looking down into from a mountain top, and watching a lazy brook meander its way through the valley, relaxing you more and more as you watch its slow movements. Another way is to imagine yourself descending a flight of stairs very slowly, while thinking to yourself as you wind down the ancient stone stairwell that you are going deeper and deeper and deeper with each step. The following script is an example of deepening the hypnotic trance state:

I want you to imagine that you are standing on the fifth floor of a large department store...and that you are just stepping into the elevator to descend to street level. And as you go down and as the elevator door opens and closes as you arrive at each floor... you will become more and more deeply relaxed... and your sleep will become deeper and deeper.

The doors are closing now...and you are beginning to sink slowly downward.

The elevator stops at the fourth floor...several people get out...two more get in...the doors close again

- ...and already you are becoming more and more deeply relaxed...more and more deeply asleep.

- And as you sink to the third floor...and stop, while the doors open and close again...you are relaxing more and more...and your sleep is becoming deeper and deeper.

- You slowly sink down to the second floor...one or two people get out and several get in...and as they do so...you are feeling much more deeply relaxed... much more deeply asleep.

- Down once again to the first floor...the doors open and close...but nobody gets out or in. Already you have become still more deeply relaxed...and your sleep still deeper and deeper. Deeper and deeper asleep...deeper and deeper asleep.

- Down further and further...until the elevator stops at last at street level. The doors open...and everybody gets out.

- But you do not get out.

- You decide to go still deeper...and descend to the basement.

- The elevator doors close again...and down you go...down and down...deeper and deeper...and as you arrive at the basement...you are feeling twice as deeply and comfortably relaxed...twice as deeply asleep.

As you develop skill with your own mind, you will be able to go into hypnosis much more quickly and even surroundings that used to be too distracting for you to handle will now become tolerable for practicing self-hypnosis.

With subsequent hypnotic sessions, you will easily learn how to develop these relaxed states. The more exposure you receive, the easier and better it will be for you.

2

THE PROCESS

In chapter 1, we observed that every year of our lives we spend 2,500 hours in natural hypnosis. This affords us a tremendous opportunity to grow spiritually, if only we know how to maximize this state. The purpose of this chapter is to show you how we can attain this goal.

Today, most hypnosis involves behavior modification and employs some form of visual imagery. It is not necessary to be able to visualize to take advantage of the superconscious mind tap technique presented in this chapter. Because the superconscious mind tap eliminates the true cause of an issue, it is not behavior modification.

CLEANSING

The basis of this process of spiritual growth through hypnosis is what I term "cleansing." Cleansing is simply the introduction of the subconscious mind to the subject's superconscious mind (higher self). It doesn't really matter what the subject is thinking about during this procedure because visualization is not necessary.

The superconscious mind is the perfect form of our subconscious mind. It is a remnant of the God energy and it is what our subconscious will eventually merge with when we perfect ourselves and ascend to the higher planes.

When the subject's subconscious mind (which is compromised and far from perfect) is exposed to the superconscious mind (which is perfect) only three things may theoretically occur. First, the subconscious may lower its energy (frequency vibrational rate). However, this is impossible, because no matter how difficult life's challenges are, your subconscious can never lower its level. If that were to occur it would literally be impossible to grow spiritually, as the world appears to possess more negativity than positiveness.

The second option is that nothing changes. I call this "plateauing." Your subconscious mind's level remains unchanged; this often happens in the early stages of hypnotherapy. Last, your subconscious mind can experience an increase in its frequency vibrational rate and raise its level to a higher value. This is the basis of the superconscious mind tap and it results in a permanent energy change.

I stated earlier that it was impossible for the subconscious to lower its level. Once you raise your energy level (this is a qualitative, not quantitative, increase), you have established a new baseline. For example, let's assume you smoke. By using this cleansing procedure you now raise your subconscious energy level to a level above the need to smoke, resulting in your permanently eliminating your previous smoking habit.

These changes are eternally permanent. Not only will you not lower your soul's energy to a previous baseline in this life, but neither will you in a future incarnation. When you cross into spirit, the subconscious mind will eventually reincarnate with the exact same energy level it manifested at the end of its previous life. Physical death has no effect on your subconscious mind frequency vibrational rate.

This cleansing takes place mostly during the REM (dream) cycle when we sleep. The reason for this is quite simple. The only real antagonist to our spiritual growth is our defense mechanisms (conscious mind proper) that exist even during our experiences with natural hypnosis during the day. The only time we rid ourselves of these defense mechanisms is when we sleep. Since the REM cycle is an alpha level, where there are no defense mechanisms present, this affords us an ideal opportunity to initiate cleansing.

We spend three hours every night in REM. The superconscious mind tap is designed to train you to spend at least one of these three hours communicating with your higher self. Every minute you spend in alpha is equivalent to three or four earth minutes, so this hour results in between three and four hours of intense spiritual growth nightly.

You may ask, why doesn't this happen naturally, without your having to do a superconscious mind tap? Throughout the day we are exposed to much stress. The REM cycle is conditioned to do emotional cleansing, without which we would die of a heart attack. Emotional cleansing is necessary for life preservation. A superconscious mind tap does not interfere with this emotional cleansing, it merely superimposes an energy cleansing on top of it.

Nature doesn't incorporate superconscious mind taps as part of our REM cycle because they are not necessary for the preservation of life. The quality of life (spiritual growth) is not one of nature's priorities. Nature only cares about keeping a species alive and facilitating its ability to reproduce to prevent extinction.

An issue may present itself in three levels. Pain would be a good example of the physical level. Let us assume the discomfort has no organic (medical) cause—but is due to a feeling of guilt—

the emotional level. The emotions may very well bring about "psychosomatic" pain; this has been accepted by modern medicine since the 1930s.

The true cause of an issue is not this emotional level. It is the soul's energy that directs the emotions that influence our physical body. By raising the frequency vibrational rate of our subconscious mind through accessing our superconscious mind, we can permanently eliminate this pain. The only level I am concerned with when I work with a patient is the energy level. Figure 1 illustrates this paradigm.

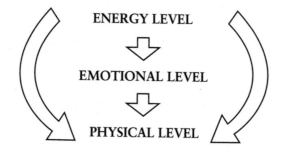

ENERGY LEVEL

EMOTIONAL LEVEL

PHYSICAL LEVEL

Figure 1

The arrows always move from the energy level down to the physical. In the case of pain, it is often not even necessary to deal with the emotional level as an intermediary. The energy level can directly affect the physical, as noted in Figure 1.

I have presented this description to prepare you for what may sound like a radical statement. The data from past life regressions, age progressions, and future life progressions do not cause a problem. This is not an analytical approach to therapy but an experiential one. The whys of an issue are irrelevant. The only prerequisite for a successful resolution of an issue is a motivated subject and a goal that is possible to attain. As long as the subject raises their subconscious energy level, the likelihood of achieving this goal improves. It doesn't even matter if they understand this process. It only matters that they raise their energy.

GOOD DAYS VS. BAD DAYS

Subjects assume that having a series of good days or weeks indicates that they are improving. In actuality, bad days are more therapeutic. While the subconscious is raising its energy, the defense mechanisms must exert more energy in an attempt to prevent this change. This drains their resources, which are limited.

The subconscious, because it is now accessing the superconscious mind, has an unlimited supply of energy to grow spiritually. We want the defense mechanisms to burn themselves out as quickly as possible. Good days mean that these defense mechanisms are saving their energy. This will not burn them out.

Fortunately, these bad days have a short life span and eventually the subject experiences one good day after another on their way to permanently resolving an issue and growing spiritually.

There are several applications to a superconscious mind tap. These are:

- Receiving spiritual guidance from your higher self or Masters and Guides.

- Scanning past lives, the future of your current lifetime, and future lifetimes.

- Contacting departed loved ones.

- Removing attached entities.

- Gaining ritual protection from negative projection techniques.

- Contacting the souls of unborn children.

SUPERCONSCIOUS MIND EXERCISE

The following script will guide you to your superconscious mind (higher self):

Now listen very carefully. I want you to imagine a bright white light coming down from above and entering the top of your head, filling your entire body....See it, feel it, and it becomes reality...Now imagine an aura of pure white light emanating from your heart region, again surrounding your entire body, protecting you....See it, feel it, and it becomes reality....Now only your higher self and highly evolved loving entities who mean you well will be able to influence you during this or any other hypnotic session...You are totally protected by this aura of pure white light.

In a few moments, I am going to count from 1 to 20. As I do so you will feel yourself rising up to the superconscious mind level where you will be able to receive information from your higher self....Number 1 rising up. 2, 3, 4 rising higher. 5, 6, 7, letting information flow. 8, 9, 10, you are halfway there. 11, 12, 13, feel yourself rising even higher. 14, 15, 16, almost there. 17, 18, 19, number 20 you are there....Take a moment and orient yourself to the superconscious mind level.

PLAY NEW AGE MUSIC FOR 1 MINUTE

You may now ask yourself questions about any past, present, or future life issue. Or, you may contact any of your guides or departed loved ones from this level. You may explore your relationship with any person. Remember, your superconscious mind level is all knowledgeable and has access to your akashic records.

Now slowly and carefully state your desire for information or an experience and let this superconscious mind level work for you.

PLAY NEW AGE MUSIC FOR 8 MINUTES.

You have done very well. Now I want you to further open up the channels of communication by removing any obstacles and allowing yourself to receive information and experiences that will directly apply to and help better your present lifetime. Allow yourself to receive more advanced and more specific information from your higher self and masters and guides to raise your frequency and improve your karmic subcycle. Do this now.

PLAY NEW AGE MUSIC FOR 8 MINUTES

All right now...sleep now and rest. You did very, very well....Listen very carefully. I'm going to count forward now from 1 to 5....When I reach the count of 5 you will be back in the present, you will be able to remember everything you experienced and re-experienced. You'll feel very relaxed, refreshed, and you'll be able to do whatever you have planned for the rest of the day or evening. You'll feel very positive about what you've just experienced and very motivated about your confidence and ability to play this tape again to experience your higher self....All right now. 1, very very deep, 2, you're getting a little bit lighter, 3, you're getting much much lighter, 4, very very light, 5, awaken. Wide awake and refreshed.

■ ■ ■

3

THE HYPNOTIC ENVIRONMENT

An appropriate setting will maximize the techniques and experience of self-hypnosis. The room itself should be warm (a few degrees above normal room temperature is ideal) and the decor should be conducive to relaxation. The walls, furniture, rugs, drapes, and floor should not present a distraction. If you like incense or other fragrances, by all means have them available, but irritating or pungent odors should be eliminated.

If you are using an eye fixation induction technique, make sure the object on which your gaze will be fixed is placed higher than the chair or couch on which you will be sitting. While many of my patients like to do their self-hypnosis in bed or lying down on a couch, I recommend a comfortable chair such as a recliner instead. Your subconscious mind is preprogrammed to associate lying down with sleeping, and if you are physically tired you may very well fall asleep. Recliners do not have that association, yet are comfortable for your body.

I always use music with my patients and for my own self-hypnosis. Recording your own tapes or using professionally recorded cassette tapes is the most efficient way I know to induce hypnosis (see chapter 11). Many people like to burn a white candle in their self-hypnosis room.

Naturally, the room should be as quiet as possible. I would close the door and inform other people present in the household not to disturb you for at least thirty minutes.

I highly recommend headphones when you use pre-recorded tapes. This functions to block out extraneous noise and directs the voice of the hypnotist to the subject's subconscious mind. Other recommendations for your hypnosis room are:

- Keep a blanket by your recliner.

- Make sure you have tissues nearby.

- Place a portable cassette player close to your chair if you want to record your experience.

- A metronome, or a tape of metronome beats, makes an excellent background for inducing hypnosis. If you are working with a subject it helps you pace your voice.

HYPNOTIC AIDS SOURCES

Hypnodiscs, Books and Tapes

I highly recommend the device I use in my office. This aid is a black and green disc mounted on a stand, that spins slowly when the electronic switch is turned on. It is powered by a Synchron 60-rpm AC motor, and when switched on the disk creates the optical illusion of two spirals moving in opposite directions at the same time. It also creates an illusion of moving through a tunnel and results in rapid inductions. I do not know of a better eye-fixation device.

This aid is available through the National Guild of Hypnotists, P.O. Box 308, Merrimack, NH 03054, telephone (603) 429–9438. The Guild carries a line of hypnosis books and tapes and offers hypnosis training to the public.

Another source of hypnotic books and supplies is Melvin Powers, Wilshire Book Company, 12015 Sherman Road, North Hollywood, CA 91605.

A west coast group that also trains the public in hypnosis and has a complete inventory of hypnosis books and aids is the American Institute of Hypnotherapy, 16842 Von Karman Ave., Suite 475, Irvine, CA 92714, telephone (800) 634-9766.

If you are the do-it-yourself/mechanical type, you could enlarge the drawing below, mount it on a stiff cardboard or thin plywood disk, and devise a way of setting it spinning.

Figure 2

New Age Music

For New Age and special background music tapes, you might contact Steven Halpern, 620 Taylor Way #14, Belmont, CA 94002.

Other New Age composers are Jon Shore, Georgia Kelly, and Kitaro.

Other Aids

For electronic aids such as alpha brain wave synchronizers, you might contact, Schneider Instrument Co., Gross Point Medical Center, 9631 Gross Point Road, Skokie, IL 60076.

You can buy metronomes in any store that sells musical instruments. This item comes in either wind-up or electronic models. Some of the latter have a red light at the top in addition to the audio beat and are made by the Franz Manufacturing Company located in New Haven, Connecticut.

Electronic supply outlets such as Radio Shack carry inexpensive tie-clip and tie-pin microphones, portable cassette players, tape decks, headphones, and pillow speakers (for listening to tapes while you sleep).

Another device for eye-fixation hypnotic inductions, the Zenon Strobe, Model 1090, is available from Data Display System, 350 East Tioga Street, Philadelphia, PA 19134. However, do not use this device if you suffer from a seizure disorder.

4

THE PRINCIPLES
OF HYPNOSIS

Before I present specific concepts of hypnosis to assist
you in making your own experimental tapes, a summary of this state of mind is in order. Hypnosis/self-hypno-
sis is a perfectly safe programming, exploratory, or
relaxation technique that can benefit anyone. It is the ultimate means of heightening motivation by programming
your subconscious mind to work in cooperation with your
conscious desires.

In chapter 2, I presented an overview of the phenomenon we call hypnosis and showed you how natural it is.
You are already familiar with hypnosis, although you may
not realize it. You go through these altered states of consciousness, or alpha brain wave levels, a minimum of twice
a day when you are crossing over into sleep and when you
are awakening.

Just think of hypnosis as an alpha brain wave state.
Most of us are capable of achieving a light-medium trance

CLINICAL CHARACTERISTICS OF BRAIN WAVES

		Brain Waves	Mental Characteristics	Physical Characteristics	Graph of Brain Waves
		100	wide awake state	extreme tension, uptight	
		95	excitement, frustration	high metabolic behavior	
		90	aware of all senses	hands moist and clammy	
		85	very alert	accelerate work ability	
	B	80	actively aware	hyperactive	
14 to 30	E	75	active thought patterns	high degree of stamina	
cycles	T	70	comfortably alert	comfortable, restful state	
per	A	65	consciously aware	good observation state	
second		60	normal thought patterns	physically at rest	
		55	easy thoughts	beginning to relax	
		50	less active thoughts	increased composure	

Figure 3

CLINICAL CHARACTERISTICS OF BRAIN WAVES— Figure 3, cont'd

		Brain Waves	Mental Characteristics	Physical Characteristics	Graph of Brain Waves
8 to 13 cycles per second	A	45	pre-drowsiness	releasing all body feeling	
	L	40	increased susceptibility	passive awareness	
	P	35	passive awareness	numb, quiet	
	H	30	total sensory withdrawal	deep relaxation	
	A	25	low alphagenic state	complete passivity	
4 to 7 cycles per second	T	20	drowsiness	unaware	
	H	15	beginning unconscious	unaware	
	E				
	T	10	unconscious	unconscious	
	A				
.05 to 3.5 cycles per second	D	5	deep sleep state	deep sleep state	
	E	0	death		
	L				
	T				
	A				

in the mid-alpha range. Hypnosis is a narrowing and focus of our attention span to convert our conscious mind proper's beta brain wave into the alpha level characteristic of hypnosis. Remember, there are only four brain waves we are able to exhibit.

In chapter 1, I pointed out that hypnosis is a setting aside of our conscious mind proper, or *beta* brain wave level on an electroencephalograph (EEG), and communicating directly with the subconscious, *alpha* state. You may recall I briefly alluded to the other brain waves, *theta* and *delta*. Theta is associated with light sleep and represents the initial phases of becoming unconscious. When we are in a deep natural sleep and completely unconscious, we refer to this as the delta level. Although we only spend about forty minutes each night in this delta brain wave state, most of our rest is obtained here.

In discussing hypnosis, the most relevant brain wave is alpha. All four brain waves exist to a certain degree, but the dominant level for our purpose in establishing the hypnotic state is alpha.

When considering the various levels of hypnosis, just remember the three stages (light, medium, and deep). Almost everyone (ninety-five percent of the public) achieves a light trance. Approximately seventy percent of us exhibit a medium trance. Only about five percent of the population are able to achieve the deep trance level.

These three stages of hypnosis can be described as follows:

Light Trance: This stage is characterized by relaxation, lethargy, and eye catalepsy (you feel unable to open your eyes). Despite these factors, most light subjects do not feel they are in a state of hypnosis.

Medium Trance: During this level the subject can relive past or future lives in greater detail. A better rapport is established, smell and taste changes are observed, analgesia (no pain) and automatic movements are also noted. Total relaxation is achieved. This is the state I prefer my patients to be in when I work with them.

Deep Trance: Complete amnesia, positive hallucinations (seeing objects that do not exist), negative hallucinations (not able to perceive things that do exist), and an almost comatose state characterize this stage of hypnosis. Xenoglossy, or the ability to speak and/or write a foreign language that is not part of the normal consciousness of the subject, is also exhibited during this level.

Helpful Hints When Using Self-Hypnosis Tapes

1. Regular use of a tape can improve your level of trance and facilitate psychic experiences.

2. If the tape player breaks while you are in hypnosis, you will wake up spontaneously or drift off into a natural sleep from which you will awaken just as you normally do.

3. Always remember that what your mind has created can be changed. It is your thoughts from past, parallel, and future lives that have resulted in your current reality. Change your thoughts by reprogramming your subconscious and accessing your superconscious, and you change your universe!

4. You don't simply have a mind, you are mind. Practicing self-hypnosis with tapes can completely redirect your karmic purpose to a more positive and fulfilling future.

5. You cannot be hypnotized against your will. Even after a hypnotic state is achieved you will be able to hear, talk, think, act, or open your eyes at any time.

6. Even a directly proposed hypnotic suggestion cannot make you do anything against your morals, religion, or self-preservation instincts. If such a suggestion were given, you would either refuse to comply or would wake up.

7. The more intelligent you are and the better your concentration and motivation, the greater the chances for attaining all goals, spiritual and otherwise.

8. Self-hypnosis tapes can facilitate your ability to improve your self-image, overcome habits and phobias, better cope with stress, improve your immune system and slow down the aging process, and exhibit improved intuition and complete relaxation.

9. Self-hypnosis is an excellent technique for experiencing psychic phenomena. Whether it be out-of-body experiences, past/future/parallel life explorations, angel encounters, telepathy, or channeling spirits, hypnosis has no equal in extrasensory perception.

10. All of the previous factors work together in allowing you to custom design your own destiny.

FACTORS AFFECTING HYPNOSIS

A pharmacist and healer in France during the early 1900s, Emile Coué was known as "the mastermind of autosuggestion." He is known for the statement: "Day by day, in every way, I am becoming better and better." We use the term "suggestibility" to describe the ability to enter into the state of hypnosis. Our mind's normally critical defense mechanisms are significantly reduced as a result of misdirection, allowing us to accept suggestions or ideas.

Another factor in enhancing the effect of suggestibility is the rapport, or relationship between the subject and the hypnotist. The greater the rapport, the easier it will be for the subject to enter into a state of self-hypnosis. All hypnosis is self-hypnosis. The personality of the hypnotist greatly affects the rapport established.

Motivation is the most important factor affecting the ability to enter into a hypnotic trance. Too much skepticism, coupled with a lack of desire to attain a goal, will almost always result in failure, regardless of the induction technique employed.

Imagination is applied in the relaxation and conditional phases of hypnosis. Those subjects possessing greater levels of imagination will produce better imagery in visualization exercises and, in general, be more suggestible. This is also a component of my hypnosis equation.

I previously mentioned expectation in my hypnotic formula. Strong desires add to our expectation, while fears work against the ability to enter into hypnosis. One way to counteract this potential problem is to learn more about hypnosis in order to alleviate any pre-hypnosis anxiety prior to experimenting with induction techniques.

Two other factors to consider are age and concentration. Children younger than five make poor subjects. My experience suggests that the ages of eight to sixteen are ideal ages for hypnosis, but hypnosis can be successful at any age. People who exhibit greater concentration find it easier to relax and have more success with self-hypnosis.

HYPNOTIC LAWS

Emile Coué made many contributions to the field of hypnosis. The most important were the three laws he formulated.

THE LAW OF CONCENTRATED ATTENTION
An idea tends to realize itself when we focus our attention on it.

Feeling hungry after viewing a fast food commercial or becoming sexually stimulated following a heated love scene in a movie are but two examples of this principle.

THE LAW OF REVERSED EFFECT
The harder you try to accomplish something, the more difficult it is to obtain.

For example, the more concentrated effort a smoker makes at trying to stop smoking, the greater their desire for a cigarette.

Any battle between will power and imagination will be won by the latter. Try not thinking of a pink elephant! However, when both will power and imagination work together, the results are multiplied by each other, not merely the sum of the two.

THE LAW OF DOMINANT EFFECT

When you accompany a suggestion with a strong emotion, the strength of the suggestion is enhanced. Any previous suggestion will now be replaced by this suggestion-emotion combination.

For instance, let us say you have a favorite restaurant where you go every Friday evening. The pleasure and enjoyment from the food and atmosphere become a dominant suggestion. Suppose one Friday evening a new group of "regulars" begin frequenting this same restaurant. These people dislike you and make fun of your appearance and behavior. Now fear and anxiety replace your previous mindset, most likely resulting in your avoiding the restaurant.

POST HYPNOTIC SUGGESTION (PHS)

A PHS is designed to remain in effect following the termination of the trance. Commonly applied cues for the enactment of a PHS are numbers (20, 20, 20), taking deep breaths, or the use of words ("sleep," "begin," or "stop").

The usual range for the duration of a PHS is four to ten days, unless it is reinforced. We don't have to worry about this factor when applying cleansing techniques, since the rise in quality of the soul's energy results in a permanent change in the subject's spiritual growth.

For more conventional hypnotic techniques, the following script can be used to present PHSs:

You are now in so deep a sleep...that everything that I tell you that is going to happen...will happen ...exactly as I tell you.

And every feeling...that I tell you that you will experience...you will experience...exactly as I tell you.

And these same things will continue to happen to you...and you will continue to experience these same feelings...just as strongly...just as surely...just as powerfully...when you are out of trance...as when you are playing this tape.

I am now going to teach you how to go into this deep relaxation, whenever you wish to do so...even though you are no longer with me, or within the sound of my voice. All you have to do is to lie back in a chair...or just say to yourself the number 20 three times, 20, 20, 20.

As you do so...your eyes will rapidly become more and more tired...your eyelids heavier and heavier...and the moment you have reached the third number 20...your eyes will close immediately...and you will immediately enter into hypnosis...just as deep as this one.

While you are in trance...stage by stage, you will be able to suggest complete relaxation of all the muscles of your body...exactly as I do...and all other suggestions that you give yourself for your own good...will act...just as effectively as if I had given them to you, myself. Should any unexpected emergency arise during your deep trance...you will automatically wake

- up immediately...fully prepared to take any neces-
- sary action.

- After you have given yourself treatment...as soon as
- you are ready to come out of trance...you will count
- slowly up to five...and the moment you reach the
- count of five...your eyes will open...and you will be
wide awake again...feeling much better than when
you went into hypnosis.

Other Principles to Consider

1. All suggestions should be worded positively and must represent attainable goals.

2. In the beginning, concentrate on one goal at a time when using self-hypnosis.

3. Begin your suggestions with simple goals first. Reserve the more difficult tasks for the end of your session or tape.

4. Always design your script to establish a definite rhythmical pattern with appropriate repetition.

5. Suggestions need to be clear, unambiguous, simple, nonthreatening and should conform with the known behavior, habits, and thoughts of the subject. To ensure success, attach an appropriate emotion to your suggestions.

6. Whenever possible, expand on a sensation that you are experiencing while you are giving yourself suggestions. For example, "with each breath that you take, your breathing will become deep, regular, and slow, and you will become even more relaxed." This approach is applied with all types of trance induction and deepening techniques.

7. Use permissive suggestions rather than authoritative commands.

8. Always allow enough time for a suggestion to be incorporated by the subconscious. It is better to refer to the immediate future, rather than the immediate present. "You will gradually develop more and more confidence in yourself" is far better than pressuring yourself by stating, "I am 100 percent confident about everything I do now."

9. Always incorporate a cue for ending a post-hypnotic suggestion if it is desired to eventually terminate it. Don't inadvertently refer to this cue if this post-hypnotic suggestion should not be ended.

Formulating Suggestions

When considering the specific wording for self-hypnotic suggestions, always emphasize the desired result, not undesirable potentials. For instance, suppose you were trying to lose weight but exhibited anxiety or nervousness, and became generally upset when you weighed yourself.

The key to your reaction lies in the words "anxiety," "nervousness," and "upset." A simple list of these words, along with their antonyms, will illustrate how to word your suggestions:

Reaction	Antonym
Anxiety	Relaxed
Nervousness	Calm
Upset	Tranquil

The appropriate suggestion using the antonym can be formed: "Whenever I weigh myself, I am relaxed, calm, and tranquil."

Using the antonym principle, consider the following negative judgments, beliefs, addictive thinking, and irrational fears, and construct your own suggestions to counteract the negative statements.

Negative Judgments

I am not good enough. I am bad, evil, or unforgivable.

I am stupid. It's always my fault.

I am a victim. I am cursed.

I am a loser. I am ugly, fat, a jerk (anything negative). Something is wrong with me.

I am not wanted (or I am abandoned).

Just when things are going good, something (someone, I) always screws it up. Time is running out.

I can't trust anyone. People take advantage of me.

I am not lovable. I am not worthy. I don't deserve anything good or better. Nobody cares about me. Nobody listens to me.

I am only loved if I'm there for them when they want and need me. As soon as I express my needs, they're gone.

The world is a cruel place and you have to continuously watch out for yourself. Grab or get it while you can. It's never going to be any different, better, or change.

Life is unfair or "After all I've done for you, this is how you treat me?"

The only thing men want is sex. The only thing women want is my money.

Irrational Beliefs

I need everyone's love and approval. I should be able to do everything well.

It is easier to avoid difficult things than to try them and risk failure.

I will enjoy life more if I avoid responsibilities and take what I can get now.

Some people are bad and should be punished.

When things aren't going well in my life, it is terrible.

If things go wrong, I'm going to feel bad, and there is very little I can do about those feelings.

People and things should be different and perfect solutions should be found.

Addictive Thinking

I am separate from everybody else. I am alone, in a cruel world.

If I want safety, I must judge others and be quick to defend myself. Attack and defense are my only safety.

For me to feel good, I have to be right. For me to feel good, I need to be perfect.

The past and the future are real and need to be worried about.

Guilt is inescapable. Fear is real.

Mistakes call for judgment and punishment, not correction and learning.

Other people are responsible for how I feel. Situations determine my experiences.

In order to win, some have to lose. Another's loss is my gain.

I need someone or something outside of myself to be complete and happy.

My self-esteem is based on pleasing you.

I can control other people's behavior.

Irrational Fears

Fear of rejection. Fear of abandonment.

Fear of being hurt again.

Fear that _____ will never happen. Fear that _____ will happen or happen again.

Fear of losing control. Fear of losing identity.

Fear of losing independence or freedom.

Fear of being smothered.

Fear of wasting more time, energy, money on a hopeless venture.

Fear of committing and then finding someone or something even better.

Fear of making decisions, commitments.

Fear of having an awful marriage, job, life like your parents, friends or _____.

Fear of responsibility. Fear of assuming financial or other responsibility for anyone else.

Fear of facing yourself. Fear of being alone.

Fear of being noticed. Fear of not being noticed.

Fear of success. Fear of failure. Fear of disease.

Fear of being found out. Fear of always having to measure up.

Fear of other people's jealousy or anger if you are too visible or successful.

Positive Statements

To assist you in formulating opposite statements representing positivity, consider these examples:

I am more than good enough to deserve _____.

I am wanted and needed by this world for the unique contribution I can make.

I am lovable. I am precisely the right sex for me.

Good things happen to me all the time (or more and more frequently).

Life gets easier and easier. I am in the flow of life.

I am surrounded by wonderful people. I make friends wherever I go. People are basically good.

You get what you give in life. What goes around comes around.

The good lives on.

Honesty is still the best policy. Integrity is rewarded.

There's more than enough (love, money, food, praise, etc.). There's increasingly more _____.

Somehow everything always turns out all right. Things work out for the best. Things just keep getting better and better.

I only need to do the important things well.

I take care of things as they come up. Failure is only feedback. I learn and move on.

People are people. They are what they are, and I accept them as I find them.

If things go wrong, I may feel bad temporarily, but I learn and move on.

I bring into the present only what I want. The past is past. The future is not here yet. Only the present moment is real.

The only person's approval I need is my own. What I see in others is a reflection of myself (or my own state of mind).

Love needs no defense. Love is unconditional.

My self-worth does not depend on my performance. I am worthy because I am. Mistakes call only for correction and learning.

I am always connected to the source of my good. I have everything I need already within me.

All the help, all the answers, all the love I need is already within me.

I am the source. No one or nothing can take away my good.

Only love is real. I am complete right now.

RELEASING FORMULA

There is a technique known as "releasing" that allows you to remove negative patterns of behavior and programming out from your psyche and replace them with positive ones.

The releasing formula is as follows:

> **I release all need to believe that** (negative judgment/belief/addictive thinking/irrational fear).

> **I now choose to believe that** (positive statement).

Or you might say, "If ever it was your experience that life was hard, let's release that belief now and know that your new experience is going to be that life is becoming easier and easier. If ever you had experienced life as a struggle, now you are going to experience life more as a flow, perhaps even as an exciting adventure. You may know of people who already experience life in this way. Now you, too, are going to learn whatever you need to learn to release whatever you need to release to enjoy life more than ever before."

You can follow up on this releasing approach with specific positive programming directly to your subconscious, with the added help of your higher self.

The following suggestions may be used to facilitate your spiritual growth to the level of a fulfilled and empowered soul. If you are making your own tapes substitute the word "I" for "you" and "my" for "your."

Your mind is now safely and peacefully identifying any occurrence in your past that may be preventing you from enjoying your life and your body to its fullest. You may now step inside your mind and cleanse and heal this memory in a beautiful color-filled light that frees you from any despair that this memory formerly had for you. Feel yourself now moving freely toward love, happiness, and fulfillment.

You eat only the correct amount of healthy foods that will encourage your ideal body weight and maximum health condition. You exercise frequently and appropriately. You notice that as you eat the correct amount of healthy food and exercise regularly you feel vital and alive, and you look younger and more attractive.

You are now releasing your own vitality. You feel vitality coursing through your body. All the energy centers in your body are open and resonating and pulsating.

- You are becoming less and less inhibited about appropriately expressing your pleasures to those toward whom you feel affection.

- You are now able to communicate your needs to others in a pleasant way that makes others want to respond to those needs.

- Each day you are becoming more and more excited by your own life and you appropriately express this loving and happy feeling.

- You are now moving away from old thought processes that impair your ability to enjoy your life and your body to its fullest.

- You are now on a fruitful, prosperous course. Each day you gain more and more momentum toward achieving your goals.

- Each day your levels of health, happiness, peace, and success increase. All your capacities are expanding.

- Feel yourself now turning on your personal power button. Feel yourself now turning on your creativity.

- You now actively draw from your subconscious any talents and strengths that have been dormant inside it.

- You now are able to disregard old thought processes and negative traits that have had adverse effects on you.

- You have become your own best friend, your own guardian angel—a cheerleader for your own success. You consistently treat yourself in a loving and respectful manner.

- You take time to notice all the wonderful, positive things you are doing with your life.

- Notice now that there is a warm, glowing light radiating from your heart and that this light is your joy—it is shining brighter each day. Feel this light moving through every cell, fiber, and nerve of your body.

- Your mind is clear. Your heart is full. Your body heals. Your soul is free and you are happy.

- Each day you will fall more in love with the world around you as you fall more in love with yourself.

- Now that you are inside this higher plane of awareness you may clearly identify any obstacles that have been standing in the way of your success. Feel yourself gaining the power and courage to move the obstacles out of your way.

- See yourself feeling happier and healthier with each step that you take toward your total fulfillment.

- You notice that you are becoming more positive about your success and more excited about yourself as you continue to take on the thoughts, deeds, and actions of a happy, healthy, and fulfilled person. You now consistently think clearly and act in your own best interest and in the best interest of humankind. You always know when to act and when to wait.

- You communicate with those around you perfectly and lovingly.

- You notice the beauty in nature around you and it heals and nourishes you.

- You turn every situation into a situation that is productive.

- You operate inside the flow of the universe, knowing that when you are operating inside the flow and for the good of humankind the universe will provide you everything that you need for support.

I presented the script for the superconscious mind tap in chapter 2. Here is a modified version that can be used for any issue:

Now listen very carefully. I want you to imagine a bright white light coming down from above and entering the top of your head....Filling your entire body....See it, feel it and it becomes reality....Now imagine an aura of pure white light emanating from your heart region....Again surrounding your entire body....Protecting you....See it, feel it, and it becomes reality....Now only your Higher Self, Masters and Guides, and highly evolved loving entities who mean you well will be able to influence you during this or any other hypnotic session. You are totally protected by this aura of pure white light.

In a few moments I am going to count from 1 to 20. As I do so you will feel yourself rising up to the superconscious mind level where you will be able to receive information from your Higher Self and Masters and Guides. You will also be able to overview all of your past, present, and future lives. Number 1 rising up. 2, 3, 4 rising higher. 5, 6, 7, letting information flow. 8, 9, 10, you are halfway there. 11, 12, 13, feel yourself rising even higher. 14, 15, 16, almost there. 17, 18, 19, number 20 you are there. Take a moment and orient yourself to the superconscious mind level.

PLAY NEW AGE MUSIC FOR 1 MINUTE

You are now in a deep hypnotic trance and from this superconscious mind level there exists a complete understanding and resolution of _____.

You are in complete control and able to access this limitless power of your superconscious mind. I want you to be open and flow with this experience. You are always protected by the white light.

At this time I would like you to ask your Higher Self to explore the origin of _____.

Trust your Higher Self and your own ability to allow any thoughts, feelings, or impressions to come into your subconscious mind concerning this issue. Do this now.

PLAY NEW AGE MUSIC FOR 3 MINUTES

Now I would like you to let go of this situation, regardless of how simple or complicated it may seem. At this time I want you to visualize yourself in your current life and consciousness free of this issue. Perceive yourself in your daily life now, completely empowered and free of this obstacle to your soul's growth. Do this now.

PLAY NEW AGE MUSIC FOR 4 MINUTES

You have done very well. Now I want you to further open the channels of communication by removing any obstacles and allowing yourself to receive information and experiences that will directly apply to and help better your present lifetime. Allow yourself to receive more advanced and more specific information from your Higher Self and Masters and Guides, to raise your frequency and improve your karmic subcycle. Do this now.

PLAY NEW AGE MUSIC FOR 4 MINUTES

All right now....Sleep now and rest....You did very, very well....Listen very carefully....I'm going to count forward now from 1 to 5....When I reach the count of 5 you will be back in the present...you will be able to remember everything you experienced and re-experienced...you'll feel very relaxed and refreshed, you'll be able to do whatever you have planned for the rest of the day or evening...you'll feel very positive about what you've just experienced and very motivated about your confidence and ability to play this tape again to experience the super-conscious mind level....All right now...1 very very deep, 2 you're getting a little bit lighter, 3 you're getting much, much lighter, 4 very, very light, 5 awaken. Wide awake and refreshed.

■ ■ ■

5

INDUCTION TECHNIQUES

W e can easily produce a hypnotic state by the constant repetition of a series of monotonous, rhythmical, sensory stimuli. These may be auditory, visual, or tactile; the key is to produce sensory fatigue.

Auditory Stimuli

The use of words such as *heaviness, sleep, drowsiness,* and *tiredness* in a monotonous, rhythmical, and persuasive manner is most effective in inducing hypnosis. Playing New Age music in the background reinforces this technique.

Visual Stimuli

Classically, the subject is told to stare at a fixed object or point, with the eyes looking up in a strained position. This results in fatigue and eventual closing of the eyes. Also produced at this time are a narrowing of attention and focused concentration.

A moving metronome, flickering lights, candles, hypnodiscs, and swinging pendulums are objects that can be used successfully to bring about this type of induction.

Tactile Stimuli

Hypnotic inductions can be initiated by gently stroking the skin. The forehead and back of the hand are the areas most commonly used with this method.

APPROACHES TO HYPNOTIC INDUCTIONS

There are two methods to initiate hypnosis. It is your own personality that will determine which one works best in your case.

Passivity of Mind with Distraction

In this approach you simply tell yourself not to listen to your tape, or the hypnotist. While the induction is proceeding, you are to engage in some mental task to occupy your mind and remove your focus from the induction mechanism. The subconscious will now be more accessible, and a faster and easier induction will ensue.

Active Participation with Attention

In this technique you are encouraged to pay strict attention to what is being verbalized and what is taking place. You are advised to focus your attention on everything that is happening, including all feelings and sensory awareness, during the induction.

The following scripts illustrate several types of induction techniques. Try each of these methods and select the one that you feel most comfortable with.

Eye Fixation Induction

I want you to lie back comfortably in the chair.

Look upward and backward at a spot on the wall. Don't let your eyes wander from the spot for a single moment.

Now start counting slowly backward, from 100... mentally, to yourself...not out loud.

Keep on counting...slowly and rhythmically...and go on counting until you hear me tell you to stop.

Try not to listen to me...any more than you can help. You will still hear everything I say...but try not to listen...just stick to your counting.

Let yourself go completely...limp and slack.

Breathe quietly...in...and out.

And while you're breathing quietly...in...and out... you can feel that your eyes are becoming very, very tired.

They may feel a little watery...the spot may begin to look a little blurred.

Already, your eyelids are beginning to feel very, very heavy and tired. Presently, they will want to blink.

As soon as your eyelids start to blink...just let them blink as much as they like.

Just let everything happen...exactly as it wants to happen. Don't try to make it happen...don't try to stop it from happening.

Just let everything please itself.

- Presently, your blinks will become slower...and bigger. And as they do so...your eyes will become more and more tired.

- The eyelids...heavier...and heavier.

- So heavy...that they feel they are wanting to close.

- As soon as they feel they want to close...let them go...just let them close...entirely on their own.

- They're wanting to close, now...let them go...closing tighter and tighter...tighter and tighter.

- Relax completely...and give yourself up completely to this very pleasant...relaxed...drowsy feeling.

- Stop counting now.

- Just relax...very, very deeply relaxed.

Eye Fixation with Progressive Relaxation

- Focus at a spot directly above your forehead. Keep staring at it. As you keep staring at the spot, the first sensation that you will learn how to control is that of heaviness. Your lids are getting very, very heavy. Getting heavier and heavier. Your eyes are beginning to blink. Your eyes are blinking and you just swallowed, that's a good sign that you are going deeper and deeper into relaxation. And now at the count of 3 you will gently control the closing of your lids. At this point you will notice that you want to close your lids because they are getting very, very tired. Precisely at the count of 3 you will close your lids, not because you have to but because you really want to.

Number 1, closing your eyes. Number 2, they are becoming tightly closed. Number 3, now they are so tightly closed that you cannot open them.

Now let your eyeballs roll up into the back of your head. Now let the eyeballs roll back down into their normal position. As they return to their normal position you will notice that your lids are stuck even tighter and tighter together.

Now I'd like to have you imagine that your entire body, from your head to your toes, is becoming very, very relaxed. Focus all your attention on the muscles in the toes of both of your feet. Imagine this warm, relaxing feeling spreading and surrounding the muscles of the toes of both feet, moving to the backs of both feet and to the heels and ankles. Now imagine this warm feeling moving up the calf muscles of both legs to the knee cap and into the thigh muscles, meeting at the hip bone.

The warm, relaxing feeling is moving up the backbone to the middle of the back, surrounding the shoulder blades and moving into the back of the neck.

The warm, relaxing feeling is now moving into the fingers of both hands, just like it did with the toes. This feeling now spreads into the back of both hands, palms, wrists, forearms, elbows, shoulders, and neck relaxing each and every muscle along its path.

The warm, relaxing feeling now moves into the intestines, stomach, chest and neck muscles.

This warm, relaxing feeling moves into the back of the head, scalp, and all the way to the forehead.

Now the facial muscles are relaxed; now the eyes (which are closed), bridge of the nose, jaws (the teeth are separated), chin, ear lobes, and neck. Now each and every muscle in the entire body is so completely relaxed.

Progressive Relaxation

Just sit back in the chair now and relax, and let yourself be comfortable. Just close your eyes, listen to my voice, focus in on what I am saying, and let yourself relax. One of the best ways to begin to relax is to take a few moments, focus in, and concentrate on your breathing. Get in tune with your entire breathing process...think about it, sense it, feel it, experience it. Sense and feel air coming into the body as you inhale; sense and feel some air leaving the body as you exhale; begin to feel the relaxation, particularly in the chest muscles, each time you exhale. Also note the nice rhythm produced each time you inhale and exhale...a very comfortable, relaxing rhythm...much like a metronome...just inhaling and exhaling. As this very normal breathing process continues, you will find that you are able to relax more thoroughly and more comfortably, and as I continue to talk with you, your breathing will assist you in relaxing even more deeply...even more completely...and at the same time I would like you to focus your attention on the top part of your head...your scalp...much like you did with your breathing, get in tune and in touch with your scalp, feelings in your scalp, sense and feel the muscles, the skin tissue, the hair follicles, and pay particular attention to the muscles of the scalp, allowing those muscles to become just as comfortable and just as relaxed and smooth as you would like.

Let that feeling of smoothness and comfort and relaxation just filter through all of the muscles in the scalp, and then just as if you were taking a relaxing shower, let that feeling of comfort and smoothness and relaxation just flow down into the muscles in the forehead. Just let those muscles smooth out and become relaxed and comfortable...flowing, comfortable relaxation...now, down into the muscles of the forehead, the temples, the cheeks, down into the chin, around the mouth, just all of the facial muscles now comfortably and thoroughly and more deeply relaxed...such a good feeling, and that feeling of comfort and relaxation can continue down into the muscles of the neck...the front, the back, the sides of the neck, down at the base of the neck where we get sort of tense or tight at times...flowing, comfortable relaxation across the shoulders, across the shoulders now, and down the arms, down the arms and through the elbows and forearms and the wrists and the hands...comfortably, thoroughly relaxed. The hands and sometimes even the scalp may tingle a little, may feel a little warm or a little cool; that sensation doesn't have to happen, but if it does it's very normal and natural...there is nothing to be concerned about...just enjoy the deep comfortable relaxation. Your breathing is excellent now, it has slowed down nicely, comfortably, and as that feeling of relaxation and comfortableness continues to flow down through all the muscles in the back and the sides and the chest and down into the waist...you can just sense yourself relaxing more deeply and completely, more thoroughly and more deeply relaxed...and as that feeling of relaxation and comfort comes into the waist area and down into the hips, you may sense a feeling of heaviness in the entire body, a feeling of heaviness more completely and more thoroughly relaxed, flowing, comfortable relaxation down through the hips and down the legs, down through the legs, down into the ankles, and finally into the feet...the entire body, all of the muscles in the body, thoroughly comfortable, and deeply relaxed...listening to my voice, focusing in on what I am saying, and just letting go...complete, total relaxation.

Hand-Clasp Induction

To practice this technique, sit in a chair and place your arms straight out in front of you at shoulder level. Make your arms as stiff and rigid as you can.

Clasp your hands tighter and tighter together...and you will feel your fingers gripping more and more firmly.

And as you do so...I want you to picture a heavy metal vise and imagine the jaws becoming screwed tighter and tighter together.

Now, picture that vise in your mind and concentrate on it...and as you do so, you will imagine that your

- hands are just like the jaws of that vise...becoming
- screwed up...tighter and tighter together.

- As I count up to 5...your hands will become locked
- together...tighter and tighter...and when I reach the
- count of 5, they will be so tightly locked together
- that they will feel just like a solid block of
- metal...and it will be difficult or impossible for you
- to separate them. 1...tightly locked...2... tighter and
- tighter...3...very, very tight...your hands feel as if
- they are glued together...4...the palms of your
- hands are locked tightly together... 5...they are so
- tightly locked that it will be impossible for you to
- separate them until I count up to 3...the harder you
- try to separate the palms of your hands...the tighter
- your fingers will press upon the back of your
- hands...and the tighter your hands will become
- locked together.

Hand Tingling Induction

As I count to 10...you will begin to experience a
light tingling or numb feeling in your left hand.
- Focus on your left hand now...block out all distract-
- ing thoughts. 1...2...3...begin to sense this tingly
- feeling.

- 4...5...6...your left hand is limp and becoming
- heavy. 7...8...feeling almost numb. 9...10...your left
- hand is now completely tingly and numb.

- Note how strange, yet pleasant, this sensation is.
- You are now in a state of hypnosis.

In just a moment I am going to count forward from 1 to 5. When I reach the count of 5, your left hand will return to its normal state, and all tingly and numb sensations will disappear. 1...2... feeling your left hand returning to normal. 3... half way there. 4...almost there. 5...completely back to normal.

Eye Opening and Closing Induction

I want you to look at a spot on the wall. Keep your eyes fixed on that spot. I am going to begin counting. I want you to open and close your eyes with each count. Each time you open your eyes, keep them fixed closely on that spot. I will count from 1 to 10. You will find that each time you close your eyes, they will want to remain closed. Each time you open them, it will be more difficult to do so, more difficult than the last time. By the time I reach 10, your eyes will be so heavy that they will stay closed and you will be in hypnosis. 1, your eyes are open, now closed...2, open...and closed...3, open and closed...your eyes are becoming very tired now, heavier with each closing...4, open...and closed...so heavy...5, open...and closed...so hard to open your eyes, 6...so drowsy and sleepy that your eyes just don't want to open, 7, open...and closed, 8, open...and closed...it's almost impossible to keep them open, 9, open...and closed...10, open...and closed. Now keep your eyes closed, as they will not open. You are in a relaxed level of self-hypnosis.

Arm Levitation Induction

Close your eyes and get comfortable. Focus your breathing and realize how easily and quickly your breathing process can help you to relax. As I talk with you, it will be easy for you to focus on my voice and the relaxation you are feeling. Each time you exhale, you will notice that your muscles will relax more and more. Focus your attention on your right arm and hand. As you concentrate on that arm and hand, I want you to see a string attached to that arm and hand at about the wrist. Attached to that piece of string is a balloon filled with helium gas, and the balloon, any color you wish, is just floating above your wrist. Just keep concentrating on that balloon above your wrist and notice how your hand and arm begins to feel. The arm and hand feel much lighter and in a few moments the arm and hand are going to feel so light that the balloon will just help them to float upward very slowly to a comfortable level. You will notice that your fingers begin to move first, and before you know it there will be a space between your fingers and your lap. Your hand will move slowly upward to a comfortable level. Lighter and lighter with a nice feeling of floating, and as the arm and hand gets lighter and lighter, you will find yourself relaxing deeper and deeper. In just a few moments now we are going to untie the balloon and just let it float away. When you untie the balloon and let it float away, your arm and hand will become heavier and heavier, and will come down slowly to rest on your lap. At this time, your right hand will

- return to its normal state, but you will still feel
- relaxed.

- Untie the balloon and watch as it floats away. Notice
- how heavy your right hand and arm feel. Your right
- hand and arm have now returned to your lap, and
- resumed their normal state. Keep this relaxed feeling
  as part of your current awareness. Enjoy this comfortable level of hypnosis.

Sound Inductions

By simply closing your eyes and focusing your mind on certain sounds, the hypnotic induction process can be easily enhanced. The classic phrase, "Listen to the sound of the metronome. Each beat of the metronome will allow you to go deeper and deeper into relaxation."

Ticking clocks, meditation chimes and background music (I prefer New Age music) of all types will work. You may also choose environmental sounds, such as the sounds of a forest or ocean. For example, "As you listen to the sounds of the ocean waves rolling in, rolling out, you go deeper and deeper into relaxation."

You may also select the whirring sound of an air conditioning or heating unit, or even a humidifier for this approach. Here is a sample script:

Relax with your eyes closed and focus all of your attention on the gentle sound coming from the air conditioning unit. Hear the gentle, peaceful and soft
- sound, and notice how relaxed it makes you feel.
- This monotonous whirring sound is allowing you, with each passing moment, to relax your entire body and enter into a comfortable level of hypnosis.

Sanctuary Induction

Sit back, relax, breathe deeply, and send a warm feeling into your toes and feet. Let this feeling break up any strain or tension, and as you exhale let the tension drain away. Breathe deeply and send this warm feeling into your ankles. It will break up any strain or tension, and as you exhale let the tension drain away. Breathe deeply and send this feeling into your knees, let it break up any strain or tension there, and as you exhale let the tension drain away. Send this warm sensation into your thighs so any strain or tension is draining away. Breathe deeply and send this warm feeling into your genitals and drain away any tension.

Send this warm feeling into your abdomen now; all your internal organs are soothed and relaxed and any strain or tension is draining away. Let this energy flow into your chest and breasts; let it soothe you and as you exhale any tension is draining away. Send this energy into your back now. This feeling is breaking up any strain or tension and as you exhale the tension is draining away. The deep, relaxing energy is flowing through your back, into each vertebra, as each vertebra assumes its proper alignment. The healing energy is flowing into all your muscles and tendons, and you are relaxed, very fully relaxed. Send this energy into your shoulders and neck; this energy is breaking up any strain or tension and as you exhale the tension is draining away. Your shoulders and neck are fully relaxed. And the deep relaxing energy is flowing into your arms; your upper arms, your elbows, your forearms, your wrists, your hands, your fingers are fully relaxed.

Let this relaxing energy wash up over your throat, and your lips, your jaw, your cheeks are fully relaxed. Send this energy into your face, the muscles around your eyes, your forehead, your scalp are relaxed. Any strain or tension is draining away. You are relaxed, most completely relaxed.

And now float to your space, leave your physical body and move between dimensions and travel to your space, a meadow, a mountain, a forest, the seashore, wherever your mind is safe and free. Go to that space now. And you are in your space, the space you have created, a space sacred and apart. Here in this space you are free from all tension and in touch with the calm, expansive power within you. Here in this space you have access to spiritual information and energy. Here is the space where you can communicate with your spirit guides. Your flow is in harmony with the flow of the universe. Because you are part of the whole creation you have access to the power of the whole of creation. Here you are pure and free. This is your personal sanctuary.

Stay here for a few minutes and when you are ready let yourself drift up and back to your usual waking reality. You will return relaxed, refreshed, and filled with energy. And you will return now, gently and easily. Open your eyes.

6

DEEPENING TECHNIQUES

With a little practice, you will attain a certain depth of trance with regularity. It doesn't matter whether you characteristically enter into a light, medium, or deep trance level. The techniques presented in this book will work with any depth of hypnosis.

Your subconscious and superconscious minds are quite good at guiding you to the depth you need to achieve in order to facilitate your spiritual growth. Don't argue with this system, work with it. As with induction techniques, practice will result in a quick and reliable level of hypnosis. This increases your confidence in attaining self-hypnosis, and the formal procedures presented will no longer be necessary.

Once having established your comfortable level of hypnosis, it is unlikely that this depth will increase with time. Certain types of people naturally achieve greater depths of trance. Among this group are individuals who exhibit more whites of their eyes when looking up, and people who can bend their hands backward. The types of people who become factory workers, artists, musicians, military personnel, and policemen are also able to reach deep trance levels, as are people living in hot (torrid) regions, such as the French, Italians, and Spaniards.

Those individuals that traditionally find it difficult to attain more than a light level of hypnosis are German and British people, scientists, engineers, lawyers, and members of other highly analytical professions, and people who are psychotic, especially paranoid schizophrenics.

INDUCTION TECHNIQUES

Try these various techniques and select the one that works for you.

Deepening by the Use of Counting and Breathing Techniques

 Take a deep breath...fill your chest...and hold it until I tell you to "Let go."

- Now I want you to notice the tension in your chest muscles...the tension in your shoulders and upper arms. And I want you to pay particular attention to how...the moment I say "Let go"...all that tension disappears immediately...and you tend to sag limply down into the chair. Now....Let go.

- I am going to count slowly up to 5...and as I do so...you will take five very deep breaths.

- And with each deep breath that you take...each time you breathe out...you will become more and more relaxed...and your trance will become deeper and deeper.

- 1...breathe deeply...more and more deeply relaxed ...deeper and deeper into relaxation.

- 2...breathe deeper...deeper and deeper relaxed... becoming deeper and deeper in hypnosis.

- 3...breathing even more deeply...more and more deeply relaxed...more and more deeply asleep.

- 4...very, very deep breath...deeper and deeper relaxed...your trance depth is becoming even deeper and deeper.

- 5...very, very deep breath...very, very deeply relaxed...very, very deeply asleep.

- Once again...I want you to take one very deep breath ...fill your chest...and hold it until I say...Let go.

- Then...let your breath out as quickly as possible... and as you do so...you will feel yourself sagging limply back into the chair...and you will become twice as deeply relaxed as you are now...twice as deeply asleep. Now, take that very deep breath...fill your chest...hold it...(15 seconds pause)...hold it... (15 seconds pause)...hold it...(20 to 30 seconds pause) Let go.

Deepening by the Induction of Arm-Heaviness

Breathe deeply and place your left arm on the arm of your chair. Using your right hand, gently stroke the back of your left hand and arm.

- As you stroke your left arm, you will begin to sense a feeling of heaviness in your arm.

That feeling of heaviness is increasing...with every stroke of your hand.

Your arm is beginning to feel heavier...and heavier...just as heavy as lead.

You can feel it pressing down more firmly upon the arm of the chair.

And in a few moments...your arm will feel so very, very heavy...and your depth of trance will become so deep....

PLAY NEW AGE MUSIC FOR 3 MINUTES

And, as you stroke your arm in the opposite direction...you will notice that all feelings of heaviness are now leaving your arm.

It is coming back to normal...and now feels just the same as your other arm.

All that feeling of heaviness has passed away completely...and your trance has become even deeper ...and deeper.

Deepening by Limb Rigidity

Extend your left arm out horizontally at shoulder level to begin this exercise.

As you stroke your left arm...you will feel that it is becoming much stiffer and straighter.

The stiffness is increasing...with every stroke of your hand.

- You can feel all the muscles tightening up...pulling your arm out...stiffer and straighter...with every stroke of your hand...until it is beginning to feel just as stiff and rigid as a steel poker...from the shoulder to the wrist.

- Now, I want you to concentrate on a steel poker.

- Picture a steel poker in your mind.

- And as you do so...you will feel that your arm has become just as stiff and rigid as that steel poker.

- As if the elbow joint is firmly locked.

- As if there is no elbow joint there at all.

- So that it will be impossible for you to bend your arm at the elbow...until I count up to 3.

- The harder you try to bend it...the stiffer, and more rigid it will become.

- But, the moment I count 3...all the stiffness will pass away immediately...your arm will bend quite easily...and, as it does so...you will fall immediately into a deeper, deeper trance.

- Your left arm is stiff and straight...just like that steel poker.

- 1...2...3...you are now in a deep level of hypnosis.

Deepening by the Induction of Automatic Movements

Place your left elbow on the arm of the chair...and hold your arm upward, with the fingers pointing toward the ceiling. Now, using your other hand,

- take your left wrist...and move it slowly...backward and forward...backward and forward.

- As you do so...I want you to imagine that the center of a piece of cord is tied around your left wrist ...and that someone at each end of the cord is pulling your left arm...first, backward...then forward.

- Just picture that piece of cord, tied around your left wrist...pulling your left arm slowly...backward... and forward...backward...and forward. And as you do so...you will find that when you release your left wrist...it will feel as if that piece of cord is still tied to your wrist...still pulling your left arm...back-ward...and forward...backward and forward. And your left arm will go on moving...entirely on its own...backward and forward...backward and for-ward...until I tell you to stop.

- Do not try to make it move!

- Do not try to stop it moving!

- Your left arm will go on moving on its own, by itself...automatically...backward...and forward... backward...and forward...until I tell you to stop.

- Backward...and forward...backward...and forward ...backward...and forward!

- Now, stop!

- Put your left arm back...on to your lap...and as you do so...falling into an even deeper, deeper trance level.

- Very, very deeply relaxed.

Escalator Technique

See yourself standing at the top of an escalator. As you look down the escalator, you will see a soft, plush, comfortable chair. In just a moment, I will ask you to get on the escalator, and as you move down slowly, just let yourself become more comfortably and deeply relaxed. Just focus on my voice, since I will be talking with you as you go down the escalator and relax deeper and deeper. When you reach the bottom, I will ask you to just sit in your comfortable chair...totally and deeply relaxed.

Go ahead now and step on the escalator and feel the movement downward as you relax deeper and deeper. The escalator is moving slowly...about one-quarter of the way down now as you really begin to feel deeper and deeper relaxed. Almost at the halfway point now, and the shape, color, and texture of your chair become clearer and clearer as you relax deeper and deeper. Very good! Isn't that nice how much more relaxed you became as you passed the halfway point. Just moving down slowly and deeply...three-quarters of the way down and almost totally relaxed and really looking forward to sitting in your chair...just listening to my voice....Coming to the bottom now and the steps are disappearing into the floor.

As you come off the escalator, just position yourself correctly and sit down in your chair...totally and deeply relaxed.

Descending Staircase Technique

I want you to picture yourself standing on a terrace, overlooking a beautiful garden. There are five wide steps leading down to a smaller terrace...and then another five, down to the garden itself.

You are going down those steps into the garden ...and I will count each step as you go down.

As you go down each step...you will take one very deep breath...and as you breathe out...you will become more and more deeply relaxed...more and more deeply in hypnosis.

Now, just picture us standing at the top of the first flight of steps.

1...Down the first step...breathe deeply...deeply relaxed...more and more deeply relaxed.

2...Down the second step...breathe deeply...very deeply relaxed...becoming deeper and deeper in hypnosis.

3...Down the third step...deep, deep breath... more and more deeply relaxed...more and more deeply in trance....

4...Down the fourth step...breathing even more deeply...very, very deeply relaxed...your trance is becoming still deeper and deeper.

5...Down the fifth step, and on to the small terrace...deep, deep breath...very, very deeply relaxed...very, very deeply asleep.

And as you pause on the terrace...you will notice a stone pedestal supporting a bowl of flowers. You will probably like to stop and look at them. Now go down the second flight of steps into the garden.

1...Down the first step...breathe deeply...deeply relaxed...deeper and deeper in trance.

2...Down the second step...breathe deeply...very deeply relaxed...becoming deeper and deeper in hypnosis.

3...Down the third step...deep, deep breath... more and more deeply relaxed...more and more deeply in trance.

4...Down the fourth step...breathing even more deeply...very, very deeply relaxed...becoming still deeper and deeper in hypnosis.

5...Down the last step and into the garden... breathing very deeply...very, very deeply relaxed... very, very deeply in hypnosis.

Deepening by Progressive Relaxation

Take a deep breath and let it out slowly. Close your eyes and lie back comfortably in the chair.

Let yourself go...loose, limp, and slack. Let all the muscles of your body relax completely.

Breathe in and out...nice and slow.

Concentrate on your feet and ankles and let them relax. Let them relax...let them go...loose, limp, and slack.

- Soon you will be aware of a feeling of heaviness in your feet.

- Your feet are beginning to feel as heavy as lead....your feet are getting heavier and heavier.

- Let yourself go completely.

- Now let all of the muscles in your legs relax totally and completely...your legs are beginning to feel heavier and heavier.

- Let yourself go completely. Give yourself up totally to this very pleasant...relaxed...comfortable feeling.

- Let your whole body go loose, limp, and slack. Your whole body is becoming as heavy as lead.

- Let the muscles of your stomach completely relax... let them become loose, limp, and slack.

- Next the muscles of your chest and your back...let them go completely loose, limp, and slack, and as you feel heaviness in your body, you are relaxing more deeply.

- Your whole body is becoming just as heavy as lead. Let yourself sink down deeper in the chair.

- Let yourself relax totally and completely...let all of the muscles in your neck and shoulders relax...let all of these muscles go loose, limp, and slack.

- Now the muscles in your arms are becoming loose, limp, slack, and heavy...as they relax, they are getting heavier and heavier...as though your arms are as heavy as lead...let your arms go.

- Let your whole body relax completely. Your whole body is deeply and completely relaxed.

- Now a feeling of complete relaxation is gradually moving over your whole body.

- All of the muscles in your feet and ankles are completely relaxed...your calf and thigh muscles are completely relaxed...all of the muscles in your legs are loose, limp, and slack.

- And as you relax...your sleep is becoming deeper and more relaxing...the feeling of relaxation is spreading through all of your body.

- All of the muscles of your body are becoming loose, limp and slack...totally relaxed.

- Your body is getting heavier and heavier.

- You are going deeper and deeper into relaxation.

- PLAY NEW AGE MUSIC FOR 4 MINUTES

- Whenever you desire to reenter into this wonderfully relaxing state of self-hypnosis, all you have to do is say the number 20 three times: 20, 20, 20, and you feel yourself sinking down into a deep relaxation. Slowly count from 1 to 5 and when you say the number 5 to yourself, your eyes will open and you will be wide awake.

Blackboard Technique

- I want you to imagine that you can see a blackboard...and that you are standing in front of it with a piece of chalk in your hand.

- Just picture that blackboard...

- Now, as you watch that blackboard...you can see yourself writing on it with the chalk.

- You can see what you are writing...you are writing the words..."Deep Trance."

- You can see that word quite clearly. Now feel the increased relaxation and enjoy this Deep Trance.

- PLAY NEW AGE MUSIC FOR 3 MINUTES

- As you continue looking at the blackboard...you now see yourself erasing the words "Deep Trance."

- And as the words..."Deep Trance"...disappear from the blackboard...so will everything that has happened during your travel also disappear from your mind...just as if your mind were being cleaned like the blackboard.

- As soon as you can see that the word has disappeared...and the blackboard is clear and blank... your state of mind will resume its normal level of conscious awareness...

Deepening by Fractionation

Fractionation consists of asking yourself to focus on the feelings, thoughts, and sensations experienced at the moment of maximum relaxation during your trance, and then dehypnotizing yourself.

While out of trance, you are to focus on these sensations and tell yourself to go deeper upon further rehypnotization. This procedure is repeated several times until a deep level of hypnosis is achieved.

You are now so deeply relaxed...that everything that I tell you that is going to happen...will happen... exactly as I tell you.

Every feeling...that I tell you that you will experience...you will experience...exactly as I tell you.

And every instruction that I give you...you will carry out faithfully.

Now...in a few moments...I will waken you up by counting up to 5.

You will wake up...feeling wonderfully better for this long rest.

And after you have awakened...I will talk to you for a minute or two.

Then, I will ask you to lie back in the chair...and relax again.

I will then say 20, 20, 20.

And the moment you hear me say...20, 20, 20... your eyes will close immediately...and you will fall immediately into a deep, relaxed state, just as deep as this one.

1...2...3...4...5...awaken!

Review your experience for one minute.

20, 20, 20....

In a few moments...I am going to wake you up by counting up to 5.

And after you have awakened...I will talk to you for a minute or two.

- Then, I will ask you to lie back in the chair...and relax again.

- I will say 20, 20, 20.

- And the moment you hear me say...20, 20, 20... your eyes will close immediately...and you will fall immediately into a deep, relaxed state, just as deep as this one!

- 1...2...3...4...5...awaken!

- In a few moments...when I count up to 5...you will open your eyes...and be wide awake again.

- You will wake up feeling wonderfully better for this long rest.

- You will wake up feeling completely relaxed...mentally and physically...feeling quite calm and composed.

- 1...2...3...4...5...awaken!

And so on.

■ ■ ■

7

OVERCOMING RESISTANCE

There are many reasons why a particular individual resists hypnosis. This resistance could manifest while working with a hypnotherapist in hetero-hypnosis. It could also be exhibited with autohypnosis, or self-hypnosis. As I stated earlier, all hypnosis is self-hypnosis.

The typical conventional reasons for showing resistance to hypnosis are:

- Dislike or lack of trust for the hypnotherapist.
- Dislike of the techniques employed.
- Poor concentration.
- Over-anxiety (performance pressure).
- Fear of hypnosis.
- Defiance of authority.
- A need to prove superiority in control issues.

- Inadequate pre-induction discussion.

- Physical discomforts and an environment not conducive to peace and quiet.

There are also important metaphysical reasons why a subject can block hypnosis. Some of these are:

- The buried trauma to be explored is too frightening.

- Some people do not want to relinquish the secondary gain from having a problem.

- Fearful associations of going "under" (actually in) hypnosis with drowning, surgery ("under the knife"), or death.

- Past life PHS given by Mystery School priests and priestesses not allowing anyone else to hypnotize you.

- Fear of exploring past lives during which you may have been persecuted or burned at the stake for your metaphysical beliefs and/or practices.

- Unwillingness to explore a past/future life for fear that it would conflict with your religion.

- Some people feel that they should suffer in this life. They also are afraid of exploring past lives which may portray them as a perpetrator or evil person.

Resistance to hypnosis may express itself in three basic areas: resistance to the induction and/or deepening techniques; resistance during the trance itself; and post-hypnotic resistance. The best way to overcome resistance is with a thorough pre-hypnosis discussion. All of my patients are presented with a discussion reflecting the principles we have previously discussed. For those of you working independently, a complete understanding of hypnosis will alleviate most, if not all, of your potential resistance.

Always bear in mind that hypnosis is a peaceful, serene, relaxing, and voluntary state of mind. We must not confuse a lack of understanding of a suggestion with resistance. That is why, in chapter 4, I pointed out the necessity of clear and unambiguous suggestions.

Some people feel that a traumatic past life scene, or other metaphysical encounter, may be dangerous. To reassure them of safety during their hypnotic session, I use a simple PHS. When I repeat the words "Sleep now and rest," the patient is instructed to detach themselves from anything they are experiencing. This affords them with a security blanket and is quite effective in reducing resistance.

There are some classic comments and concerns reported by resistant hypnotic subjects.

Some of these are:

- **I could easily have opened my eyes if I wanted to, so how could I be in hypnosis?**

   In hypnosis you are always in control. The only reason you allowed your eyes to remain closed is because you did not want to open them.

- **I do not believe I was hypnotized because my mind was wandering. I could hear everything you said.**

   You are supposed to be aware of all that occurs during hypnosis, except in deeper trances. Most command levels of hypnosis are characterized by a hyperawareness (hearing, taste, and smell are more acute in hypnosis). Your mind will wander in any level of trance. The specific part of your mind that is doing the wandering is your conscious mind proper (defense mechanisms). We want that component of our consciousness to wander.

- **Should I be in a deeper state of hypnosis?**

   Only the subject can truly control the level of trance. Deeper trance levels are not required for metaphysical experiences or therapeutic resolution of issues. I prefer my patients to be in a light-medium trance for the majority of their session.

- **Since I couldn't do everything you suggested, does that mean that hypnosis will not be able to assist me?**

  Very few subjects respond to every suggestion while in hypnosis. It is not critical to accept each and every suggestion immediately. Simply accept what you can now and do not worry about those that for now seem beyond your grasp. This experience is perfectly normal.

- **Suppose the tape broke during my trance. Would I be trapped in a past or future life?**

  If the trance was interrupted for any reason, you would either fall asleep and wake up naturally, or simply come out of the trance in a short time by yourself. Remember, you spend four hours during your waking day in hypnosis (daydreams). You do not need anyone to bring you out of hypnosis. It is physically and metaphysically impossible to become trapped in a past, parallel, or future life.

- **I tried so hard to cooperate, but nothing seemed to happen.**

  You can create anxiety, or performance pressure, by focusing too much on the procedure or clinical goal. It is best to just relax and allow the tape or hypnotherapist to "do their thing."

In a pre-hypnosis discussion (the best way to prevent resistance) I point out the following facts concerning hypnosis:

- Anyone can allow self-hypnosis to occur. We spend seven hours each twenty-four hour day in natural self-hypnosis.

- It is the simple acceptance of certain words in the form of suggestions that comprises hypnosis.

- If you can speak and read, you can induce self-hypnosis.

- The "power" of hypnosis always rests with the subject, not the hypnotherapist. Each individual reacts to hypnosis in their own manner. When presented with their own specific experiences in this relaxing state, the induction process is facilitated.

Always bear in mind that the ego cannot be detached in hypnosis. This means that you will not relay information during a trance that you would not normally discuss (assuming no general anesthesia is administered), and your moral and ethical codes can never be violated.

IS HYPNOSIS DANGEROUS?

This fear of danger is by far the greatest obstacle to enjoying the wonderful state of mind known as hypnosis. I want to fully explore this question before presenting my response.

The late Milton Erickson pointed out years ago that many skilled hypnotists had failed in attempts to engage in sex while their wives or mistresses were in hypnosis. In each case this sexual activity resumed when these women came out of trance because they had felt "deprived by being in the trance state."[1]

Erickson emphasizes the fact that there is no evidence that hypnosis weakens a person's will or renders them any more dependent than any other therapeutic technique. There is no real danger that a hypnotized subject will act out fantasies in a properly conducted hypnotic session.

We can look to Erickson's work to note the fact that rapists' sexual delusions and fantasies do not frequently occur during hypnotic sessions. No situation has been adequately demonstrated to suggest that hypnosis could be used for the committing of any crime, either major or minor—including seduction.

There is concern that hypnosis could bring on a psychiatric illness. The fact is that the psychotic process develops slowly over a period of years and is not precipitated by one or many hypnotic sessions. In

---

1 M. Erickson, "An Experimental Investigation of the Possible Anti-social Use of Hypnosis." *Psychiatry* 2 (1939): 391–414.

my own practice, since 1974, I have treated over 11,000 individual patients with hypnosis and have never observed hypnosis "precipitating a psychiatric illness." M. K. Bowers reports hypnotherapy being successfully used to treat schizophrenia![2]

Hypnosis is most certainly not a "power" or external "force" that can coerce subjects into metaphysical servitude. It is a state of mind that is natural. The subject may assume that he or she is under the control of the hypnotist so that both may benefit from this association in a type of shared fantasy.

R. E. Shor was quite correct when he wrote, "The idea that persons in hypnosis lose their fundamental defenses and basic moral commitments is contrary to all I know of the phenomenon."[3] We have come a long way from the time when Mesmer propagated his pseudo-scientific theory, animal magnetism, which was the only available explanation of the phenomena that occurred around the baquet and the magnetized tree.[4]

During the past 175 years many thousands of patients undergoing hypnosis have been studied. In no case has hypnosis successfully been cited as the cause of any harm whatsoever to these individuals.

Outmoded Svengali-like theories derived from nineteenth-century authors of hypnosis-science fiction, isolated instances of mismanaged patients by incompetent operators, and the occasional disorganization of undiagnosed prepsychotic individuals following hypnosis simply do not establish hypnosis as a dangerous technique. It is for these and many other reasons that I state with absolute certainty, *hypnosis is not dangerous.*

---

2   M. K. Bowers, "Theoretical Considerations in the Use of Hypnosis in the Treatment of Schizophrenia." *International Journal of Clinical and Experimental Hypnosis* 9 (1961): 39–46.

3   R. E. Shor, "Three Dimensions of Hypnotic Depth." *International Journal of Clinical and Experimental Hypnosis* 10 (1962): 23–38.

4   V. Faw, D. J. Sellers and W. W. Wilcox, "Psychopathological Effects of Hypnosis." *International Journal of Clinical and Experimental Hypnosis* 16 (1968): 26–37.

8

THE ROLE OF KARMA

Karma is a Sanskrit word meaning "action," or the connection of our present circumstances with past actions. There are four aspects of karma:

- Cause and effect.
- Compensation.
- Balancing.
- Completion.

Today, most people associate karma with reward and punishment. This is the cause and effect aspect, commonly described as, "As ye sow, so shall ye reap." This karmic law of retribution states that we will be rewarded or punished as a result of our previous actions. The problem with this concept is that we are always reacting to the past. What about our new karma? This concept implies some external agent decides on our reward or punishment.

The compensation aspect of karma is characterized by our atoning for a past misdeed, by performing a good task now, or through a form of creative suffering. This principle calls for immediately paying a karmic debt before it is compounded. One problem with this method is that if too many good acts are performed, a series of negative actions will be initiated by the soul to compensate.

The balancing principle simply states that for the soul to perfect itself, it has to balance every single negative deed with a positive one. This does not have to be done immediately as with the compensation aspect. When its karmic balance sheet is zero, the soul can then ascend to the higher planes and join God.

Finally, the completion aspect is related to one subcycle. In the total karmic cycle, there are many subcycles. These subcycles represent a small cluster of several lifetimes during which lessons illustrating a limited number of principles are presented to the same group of souls.

Group karma is a feature of the completion aspect. Your parents, lover, children, and best friend may have been involved in all of these lifetimes with you. The lesson you were supposed to learn may have been patience or sacrifice. If you learned it, you go on to the next lesson. Completion occurs when you "graduate" from one subcycle (more spiritually evolved) and move on to the next one. The ultimate completion is ascension to the higher planes and God.

Karma focuses us. When we're rigid, a great deal of pain is sometimes necessary to bring us to the point of paying attention. When we give up old false patterns, the new life entering our world often feels like a conversion experience.

Karma operates through the mechanisms of the programming effect of separation or attachment. The purpose and end result of karma is not just to balance our actions, or to recover, lose, undo, or accomplish something. These are all means to the end—to perfect the soul and make it free.

When we hate someone, we attach a negative karmic aspect to our subcycle. Our natural tendency is to sublimate, avoid, or project these unpleasant feelings, eventually resulting in another karmic test.

We must remember that our choices create our karma. We choose our parents, children, the major circumstances in our lives, our race, creed, and socioeconomic status. The only person to blame for our condition in life is ourself.

Fortunately, there is a solution to our karmic cycle. We can all perfect ourselves. The laws of karma are perfectly just and we do have free will. We can incorporate the principle of forgiveness. This states that we can make up for many past negative actions by performing one positive action now and changing our behavior to reflect that positive lifestyle.

An example of the principle of forgiveness was experienced by a patient of mine who lived as a murderous pirate in sixteenth-century Spain. He killed for pleasure alone. One day, he chose not to kill a group of prisoners he had captured. Instead, he retired from that lifestyle and spent the rest of his life helping others. This resulted in a complete elimination of his negative karma from his past crimes. Karma gives us all an incentive to grow spiritually.

THE PLANE CONCEPT

Our karmic cycle is actually worked out on what is termed the five lower planes. Some schools of thought propose seven lower planes, but my patients confirm the former number. The soul is trapped within these five planes until it perfects itself. This newly perfected soul may then ascend to the higher planes, and eventually to God.

The Five Lower Planes

- **The earth plane or physical plane.** This is the plane that we function in now. The body is most material or physical at this level. The greatest amount of karma can be erased or added on at this level. This is by far the most difficult level.

- **The astral plane.** The body is less material here. This is where the subconscious, or soul, goes immediately following death or crossing over. Ghosts are examples of astral bodies.

- **The causal plane.** The body is even less material at this level. The akashic records are kept here. This is where a medium or channel projects him or herself when he or she reads your past or future.

- **The mental plane.** This is the plane of pure intellect.

- **The etheric plane.** The body is least material at this level. On this plane, truth and beauty are the ultimate values.

The amount of time spent on these lower planes depends entirely on the soul's achievements and remaining karmic debts. If you need to develop intellectually, you would select the mental plane. If truth is most important to your karmic cycle, the etheric plane would be the logical choice. The earth plane represents the plane of greatest elimination or addition to our karmic debts.

The Moment of Death

This all-important transition from the physical plane to the astral plane is characterized by telepathic communication and the presence of masters and guides who advise us. The soul enters into a white light and is joined by the higher self. Departed relatives may be present at this time. Our purpose here is to enter the white light and travel to the soul plane. If we don't do this, we may remain on the earth plane as a troubled spirit (ghost or poltergeist), or in the astral plane in limbo.

The Soul Plane

This plane functions as a buffer zone between the lower five planes and the higher planes. It is here that you will evaluate your most recent life and choose your next incarnation. Your higher self and masters and guides will advise you, but the decision is yours.

The decision process is rather complex: you are shown a panoramic overview of several of your past lives and optional future lifetimes. You may select any of the lower five planes for your next life. The earth plane affords the greatest opportunity for the removal or addition of karma. Life on these other planes isn't much different. Souls occupy a less material body, but they marry, raise children, and deal with society. The only restriction is that you cannot select the higher planes until you are perfect.

Akashic Records

The akashic records are a complete file on all of your past, present, and future lifetimes. They are reportedly stored on the causal plane (although some schools of thought differ on this location), but they may be accessed on any of the lower five planes. These records are easiest to tap into on the soul plane.

The Higher Planes

Beyond the soul plane are seven higher planes. The highest is the God or nameless plane. Others refer to this thirteenth plane as heaven or nirvana. The soul can only reside on the higher plane that matches its frequency vibration rate. For example, let us assume you want to go to the ninth plane, but your frequency vibrations rate only qualifies you for the eighth plane. In this instance, your soul would end up in the eighth plane until it raises its frequency vibration rate to qualify for the ninth plane. Your level of consciousness—thought and actions—determines your vibration rate.

The aspect of this concept that I like best is the certainty that there is no hell. Hell is merely the negativity a soul generates for itself on the earth plane. There is, however, a heaven. Figure 4 illustrates the plane concept:

THE PLANES

God or Nameless Plane		Plane 13	
Seven		Plane 12	
Higher		Plane 11	
Planes		Plane 10	
		Plane 9	
		Plane 8	
		Plane 7	
Soul Plane		Plane 6	
Karmic	Etheric Plane	Plane 5	
Cycle	Mental Plane	Plane 4	
(Lower 5	Causal Plane	Plane 3	Akashic Records
Planes)	Astral Plane	Plane 2	
	Earth Plane	Plane 1	You are here

Figure 4

Superconscious Mind Tap

A soul plane ascension is actually an advanced superconscious mind tap. It is one of the most enlightening experiences you can attain through hypnosis. The following script is one that I use in my office.

 Now listen very carefully. I want you to imagine a bright white light coming down from above and entering the top of your head, filling your entire body...See it, feel it, and it becomes reality...Now imagine an aura of pure white light emanating from your heart region, again surrounding your entire body, protecting you...See it, feel it, and it becomes reality...Now only your angels and highly evolved loving entities who mean you well will be able to influence you during this, or any other, hypnotic session. You are totally protected by this aura of pure white light.

In a few moments, I am going to count from 1 to 20. As I do so, you will feel yourself rising up to the superconscious mind level, where you will be able to receive information from your higher self...Number 1 rising up. 2, 3, 4, rising higher. 5, 6, 7, letting information flow. 8, 9, 10, you are halfway there. 11, 12, 13, feel yourself rising even higher. 14, 15, 16, almost there. 17, 18, 19, number 20, you are there...Take a moment and orient yourself to the subconscious mind level.

PLAY ASCENSION MUSIC FOR 1 MINUTE

Now from the superconscious mind level you are going to rise up and beyond the karmic cycle and the lower planes to the soul plane. The white light is always with you, and you may be assisted by your masters and guides as you ascend to the soul plane...Number 1 rising up. 2, 3, 4, rising higher. 5, 6, 7, letting information flow. 8, 9, 10, you are halfway there. 11, 12, 13, feel yourself rising higher. 14, 15, 16, almost there. 17, 18, 19, number 20, you are there...Take a moment and orient yourself to the soul plane.

PLAY ASCENSION MUSIC FOR 1 MINUTE

From the soul plane you are able to perceive information from various sources and overview all of your past lives, your current lifetime, and future lives, including all of your frequencies...Take a few moments now to evaluate this data and choose your next lifetime. Get a feel for the entire process.

PLAY ASCENSION MUSIC FOR 6 MINUTES

You have done very well. Now I want you to further open up the channels of communication by removing any obstacles and allowing yourself to receive information and experiences that will directly apply to and help better your present lifetime. Allow yourself to receive more advanced and more specific information from your higher self and guides to raise your frequency and improve your karmic subcycle. Maintain the communication and connection with your higher self. You are one with your higher self. This connection will always exist, even when the physical body dies. Allow your higher self to instruct you. Do this now.

PLAY ASCENSION MUSIC FOR 8 MINUTES

All right now...Sleep now and rest. You did very, very well...Listen very carefully. I'm going to count forward now, from 1 to 5. When I reach the count of 5, you will be back in your physical body. You will be able to remember everything you experienced and re-experienced; you'll feel very relaxed, refreshed; you'll be able to do whatever you have planned for the rest of the day or evening. You'll feel very positive about what you've just experienced and very

- motivated about your confidence and ability to enter
- into hypnosis again, to experience the soul
- plane...All right now. 1, very, very deep. 2, you're
- getting a little bit lighter. 3, you're getting much, much lighter, 4, very, very light, 5, awaken. Wide awake and refreshed.

AGE REGRESSION

Regression is simply going back in time. If you think about what you had for lunch yesterday, you are regressing with your conscious mind. Hypnotic regression is going back in time by using the subconscious mind with its perfect memory bank. I will use the term "simple age regression" to refer to going back in time in this lifetime. The term "past life regression" will refer to the going back in time in a prior lifetime.

A simple age regression subject is guided back in time by systematic disorientation to the present year, month, and day. Appropriate suggestions are then given to reach the earlier age. Personality traits characteristic of this age will often be exhibited by the regressed subject. For example, speech patterns, handwriting, and other characteristics of that earlier age become evident.

There are two types of age regression. The first type is called *revivication*. In this type, the hypnotized subject actually relives or re-experiences the events of his or her life at an earlier age. For the duration of the trance, all memories of events following the regressed age are removed. Only somnambules (subjects capable of very deep trance) are capable of achieving this deep level trance. Although it is easier to obtain desired information at this level, it is not necessary to attain this level to use simple age regression.

The second type of age regression is called *pseudo-revivification*. This type is characterized by the subject being able to relive scenes from an earlier age, but the memories following this age are not forgotten. In other words, the subject is aware that he or she is still in the present, but the scenes are from the past. Their speech, handwriting, and other characteristics will not have changed from those they currently possess. This is by far the most common form of age regression, and much detailed information can be obtained here. In this type of regression, as with any other regression, the subject will re-experience the emotions of the scenes he or she is reliving.

At no time is the subject in danger of being trapped in this earlier age. Even in true revivification, the patient can come back to the present at any time he or she wants to.

One characteristic of both types of regression is hypermnesia, or heightened recall. The memory banks of the subconscious mind are now being tapped and the subject can recall literally anything that he or she has seen, heard, touched, smelled, or tasted. As long as you physically experienced something, age regression can bring that information back. The use of hypnosis in criminal investigation has received much attention for just the reason we have been discussing: the strength of recall under hypnosis. From remembering license plate numbers to recalling the details of a rape or murder case, hypnosis has been accepted as an important evidence-gathering technique by many police departments. The fact that courts have employed the services of hypnotherapists shows that public opinion of the validity of this technique has changed. The following script will guide you back in time to an earlier stage of your current lifetime.

Now listen very carefully. In a few minutes, I'm going to be counting backward from 20 to 1 one more time. As I count backwards from 20 to 1, you are going to perceive yourself moving through a very deep and dark tunnel. The tunnel will get lighter and lighter, and at the very end of this tunnel there will be a door with a bright white light above it. When you walk through this door, you will be at an earlier age. You are going to re-experience this earlier age and move to an event that will be significant in explaining your present personality, or the origin of any problem or negative tendency. But before I do that, I want you to realize that if at any time you feel uncomfortable, either physically, mentally, or emotionally, you can awaken yourself from this hypnotic trance by simply counting forward from 1 to 5. You will always associate my voice as a friendly voice in trance. You will be able to review your mind's memory bank, perceive the scenes from this earlier age, and follow along as I instruct. You'll find yourself able to go deeper and more quickly into hypnotic trances each time you practice with this tape or other methods of self-hypnosis. When you hear me say the words "sleep now and rest," I want you to immediately detach yourself from any scene you are experiencing. You will then wait for further instructions.

You absolutely have the power and ability to go back in time, as your subconscious mind's memory bank remembers everything you've ever experienced. I want you to relive these past events only as a neutral observer, without feeling or emotion, just as if you were watching a television show. I want you to choose positive, neutral, or happy experiences. You will be able to remove any obstacles that are preventing you from achieving your most useful, positive, beneficial, and constructive goals. Go back and be able to explore at least two or three memories of yourself. It doesn't matter how far you go back. It doesn't matter what the years are. I just want you to get used to going backward in time.

I'm going to count backward now from 20 to 1. As I do so, I want you to feel yourself moving into the past. You'll find yourself moving through a pitch-black tunnel that will get lighter and lighter as I count backward. When I reach the count of 1, you will have opened up a door with a bright white light above it and walked into a past scene. You will become yourself at an earlier age once again. Now listen carefully....Number 20, you're moving into a very deep, dark tunnel, surrounded by grass and trees and flowers and a very inviting atmosphere. You feel very calm and comfortable about moving into the tunnel. 19, 18, you're moving backward in time, back, back. 17, 16, 15, the tunnel is becoming lighter now. You can make out your arms and legs and you realize that you are walking through this tunnel and you're moving backward in time. 14, 13, 12, moving so far back, back, 11, 10, 9. You're now so far back, you're more than halfway there, and the tunnel is much lighter. You can perceive objects around you and you can now make out that the door is in front of you with the bright white light above it. 8, 7, 6, standing in front of the door now, feeling comfortable and feeling positive and confident about your ability to move into this past scene. 5, 4, now walk up to the door, put your hand on the doorknob. The bright white light is so bright, it's hard to look at. 3, open the door. 2, step through the door. 1, move into the past scene. You are there.

Focus carefully on what you see before you. Take a few minutes now and let everything become crystal clear. The information is flowing into your awareness; the scene is becoming visual and visible. Just let yourself orient yourself to the environment. Focus on it. Take a few moments and then listen to my instructions. Let the impressions form.

PLAY MUSIC FOR 30 SECONDS

First, what do you perceive and what are you doing? Focus carefully on my voice now. I want you to let any information—the scene, as well as the actual environment that you are in—acknowledge the information flowing into your awareness to become clear now. Crystal clear. I want you to focus on yourself. First of all, where are you? Focus on how old you are, how you are dressed, what you are doing there, what your purpose is there at this particular time, who else is around you—parents, relatives, friends. Let the scene crystallize for a moment. I'm going to give you a few moments. I want you to let the scene develop—develop and become clear. Develop and become crystal clear.

PLAY MUSIC FOR 4 MINUTES

Sleep now and rest. Detach yourself from this scene now. I want you to focus on my voice again. I'm going to be counting forward again, this time from 1 to 5. When I reach the count of 5, I want you to progress in time by 3 years. I want you to move at least 3 more years forward in time.

Move to a specific event that is going to happen to you—something that is going to affect you and your development. I want you to move forward to a very significant scene. Especially if it involves other people. On the count of 5 now, I want you to perceive yourself in this scene just like you did before. Number 1, moving forward, carefully, comfortably, slowly. Number 2, moving further forward. Number 3, halfway there. 4, almost there. 5, you are there. Now focus again, let the scene crystallize and become clear. Focus on yourself. Where are you? Who are you with? What is happening around you? What has happened since I last spoke with you? Understand the physical setting of the scene. Let it develop. Allow it to relate to your particular problem or just to experience going back in time. Carefully, comfortably allow the scene to unfold. Carefully and comfortably. Now perceive the scene unfolding. Let it unfold now.

PLAY MUSIC FOR 4 MINUTES

Sleep now and rest. Now listen to my voice; detach yourself from this scene. We're going to be moving forward one more time now. On the count of 5, you're going to be moving forward to a minimum of 5 years from this time. You will be moving forward to the resolution to this problem, or another significant scene that will affect the development of this problem, or just an experience of going back in time again. Moving forward to a minimum of 5 years from this time on the count of 5. Carefully, comfortably. Number 1, moving forward. 2, moving further forward. 3, halfway there. 4, almost there, 5. Now, again, let the scene crystallize, become crystal clear. Focus on what is happening around you. Where are you? If this is a problem you are resolving, find out exactly what happened. Exactly how was it resolved? Find out what additional facts are related to the present problem. Carefully and comfortably let the images flow and the scene become clear.

PLAY MUSIC FOR 4 MINUTES

All right, very good, you've done very well now. Sleep and rest. Listen carefully, as I am going to count forward again from 1 to 5. On the count of 5 you will be back in the present, you will still be in a deep hypnotic trance, but you will be able to relax comfortably and be free of these scenes. Number 1, you're heading forward in time, back to the present. 2, further forward. 3, halfway there. 4, almost there. Number 5. Listen as I count forward one more time from 1 to 5. On the count of 5 you will be wide awake, refreshed, relaxed; you will be able to do what you have planned for the rest of the day or evening. You will be able to remember everything that you experienced and re-experienced, and be perfectly relaxed and at ease. You will also be able to facilitate further experiences of scenes from the past with additional playing of this tape. Number 1, very, very deep. 2, you're getting a little lighter. 3, you're getting much, much lighter. 4, very, very light. 5, awaken.

Abduction Case History

One important New Age application of age regression is in the treatment of UFO abduction ("missing time") cases. Jill's case is an excellent example of how repressed memories of her lifelong abduction experiences were uncovered.

Jill has been abducted over forty times since the age of seven. She is now in her thirties and was raised in a very conservative and traditional family where beliefs such as in UFOs were discouraged. Jill and her eight-year-old son had reported nosebleeds of unknown origin throughout their lives. This is a frequent sign in alien implant cases. She also has a three-quarter inch scar on her right calf and a scoop-type scar on her left calf. These are classically reported in abduction cases during which surgery was performed.

Her missing time episodes have been witnessed by her son and live-in boyfriend. She has had at least two pregnancies "spontaneously" disappear, baffling her physician. The most recent episode occurred in 1994.

Jill has been taken aboard UFO crafts and has observed genetic experiments being conducted, along with sheep and cattle suspended from nylon ropes. The following excerpts from her sessions describe one of her more dramatic abductions:

"My eyes closed, but this time, I was still very much aware. I felt forward movement and an intense rush of speed. Gravity fluttered in my stomach. The force of motion barely compared to that of an explosive sudden drop of a five-star theme park ride. The high-pitched whir of a thousand Porsche engines spun in my ears. I was going somewhere.

"My legs were straight out in front of me. I was moving through a small opening, feet first. I did not feel the pressure of anyone holding me. I was floating through the air! My son was floating, too, right next to me.

"We were passing through a small portal-like opening not much wider than my body. I craned my eyes to look below me, as I could not move at all. What came next changed me. I received a glance of a world wholly foreign to everything I knew and had ever learned."

Later, she described a scene in a laboratory on board this craft: "As I passed the display more closely, I could see many pinkish, human-like fetuses, at different stages of development. They were all suspended in clear liquid and encased in oval-like jars. The containers were like simulated wombs. I was relieved that this display did not contain dismembered body parts as it looked from a distance. I took a big breath. The craft continued through the air."

I have conducted age regressions on approximately one hundred UFO abductees, but Jill's case represents one of the few cases where both a mother and child were abducted together.

Jill had no awareness of these abductions until she underwent age regression hypnotherapy in my office. Jill has also done her own age regressions with my age regression conditioning tape to obtain further information about several of these abductions. Some of the abductions involved her son, but most were solo trips.

PAST LIFE REGRESSION

Past life regression refers to going back in time to review lives you lived in other time periods when you have a different physical body. This concept accepts reincarnation as the main mechanism in the evolution of our soul (subconscious mind).

We may change sexes, races, socioeconomic status, and geographical location in our previous existences. Our subconscious mind's memory bank is perfect; we all have the ability to access our akashic records and perceive our past lives.

Xenoglossy is a rare but fascinating phenomenon observed in past life therapy. This is the speaking or writing during a hypnotic trance of a foreign language that the subject has no knowledge of in the normal waking state. It is even more impressive when children exhibit this ability.

Some subjects fear that past life experiences represent a form of possession. Let me assure you that this is never the case. In cases of spirit possession it has been observed that the subject experiences a seemingly total change of personality, and appears to have been invaded by a separate entity. It is as if another soul has entered into the subject's body and is existing in place of, or side by side with, the normal soul. The change of personality in a case of a past life regression is slight or entirely absent.

In cases of possession, the subject takes on a whole new behavior. From the moment the possessing soul seizes the victim, his features change dramatically and his individuality vanishes. The voice of the possessed person also changes. The feminine voice becomes extremely low. The invading entity usually reveals a vulgar attitude, fundamentally opposed to all acceptable ethical and religious norms. In a past life regression, the subject remains his normal self. His features do not change.

When the possession occurs, the person immediately loses consciousness, the mind's ascendancy over the body ceases, and a totally new and most often hostile personality manifests itself. This is not so in the case of a past life regression. The subject retains his consciousness throughout and talks lucidly of his previous life.

There is nothing to fear about experiencing one of your past lives. My script includes white light protection, just in case you are still concerned.

There are five ways you can experience information about your past lives. The most desired type, but unfortunately not the most common form, is what I refer to as the audio-visual receiver. The subject experiences scenes in his or her mind (similar to watching a movie), accompanied by information. The most common type is one of quick and cloudy impressions. The second type consists of visual images that appear in your mind but quickly disappear. Most of the information you receive is through thoughts. The third type is entirely audio or thoughts. A sensation as if someone were whispering in your ear constitutes the fourth type. The fifth type is characterized by reading words that pass before your inner eyes. These last two types are quite rare (less than one percent of all experiences), but do not signify abnormal behavior.

Shielding or protective techniques are always applied to a patient undergoing a past life regression. I shield with what I call "spiritual protection." This technique consists of having the patient imagine a pure white light entering the top of the head and filling the entire body, surrounding each and every muscle, bone, and organ. The technique is powerful, despite being disarmingly simple. The white light protects the patient from any harm or negativity that he or she may have been exposed to in their current life. This visualization further acts as an induction technique that is most appreciated by the patient.

The following script is recommended for a past life regression.

Now listen very carefully. I want you to imagine a bright white light coming down from above and entering the top of your head. Filling your entire body. See it, feel it, and it becomes reality. Now imagine an aura of pure white light emanating from your heart region. Again surrounding your entire body. Protecting you. See it, feel it, and it becomes reality. Now only your masters and guides and highly evolved entities who mean you well will be able to influence you during this or any other hypnotic session. You are totally protected by this aura of pure white light. Now listen very carefully. In a few minutes I'm going to be counting backward from 20 to 1. As I count backward from 20 to 1, you are going to perceive yourself moving through a very deep and dark tunnel. The tunnel will get lighter and lighter and at the very end of this tunnel there will be a door with a bright white light above it. When you walk through this door you will be in a past life scene. You're going to re-experience one of your past lives at the age of about fifteen. You'll be moving to an event that will be significant in explaining who you are, where you are, and why you are there. I want you to realize that if you feel uncomfortable either physically, mentally, or emotionally at any time you can awaken yourself from this hypnotic trance by simply counting forward from 1 to 5. You will always associate my voice as a friendly voice in trance. You will be able to let your mind review its memory bank and follow the instructions to perceive the scenes of your own past lives, following along as I instruct. You will be able to go deeper and more quickly into hypnotic trances each time as you practice with this tape or other methods of self-hypnosis. When you hear me say the words "sleep now and rest," I want you to immediately detach yourself from any scene you are experiencing. You will wait for further instructions.

You have the power and ability to go back into a past life, as your subconscious mind's memory bank remembers everything you've ever experienced in all your past lives as well as in your present life. I want you to relive these past life events as a neutral observer, without feeling or emotion, just as if you were watching a television show. I want you to choose a past life in which you've lived to at least the age of thirty. I want you to pick a positive, neutral, or happy past life experience. I'm going to count backward now from 20 to 1. As I do so I want you to feel yourself moving into the past. You'll find yourself moving through a pitch-black tunnel which will get lighter and lighter as I count backwards. When I reach the count of one you will open a door with a bright white light above it and walk into a past life scene. You will once again become yourself, at about the age of fifteen, in a previous lifetime.

Now listen carefully....Number 20, you're moving into a very deep dark tunnel surrounded by grass and trees and your favorite flowers, and it is very, very inviting; you feel very calm and comfortable about moving into the tunnel. 19, 18, you're moving backward in time, back, back. 17, 16, 15, the tunnel is becoming lighter now. You can make out your arms and legs and you realize that you are walking through this tunnel and you're moving backward in time. 14, 13, 12, moving so far, back, back, back. 11, 10, 9, you're now so far back that you're more than halfway there; the tunnel is much lighter. You can see around you, and you can now make out the door in front of you with the bright white light above it. 8, 7, 6, standing in front of the door now, feeling comfortable, and feeling positive and confident about your ability to move into this past life scene. 5, 4, now walk up to the door, put your hand on the doorknob, the bright white light is so bright, it's hard to look at. 3, open the door. 2, step through the door. 1, move into the past life scene. Focus carefully on what you perceive before you. Take a few minutes now; I want you to let everything become crystal clear—the information flowing into your awareness, the scene becoming visual and visible. Orient yourself to your new environment. Focus on it. Take a few moments and listen to my instructions. Let the impression form. First, what do you see and what are you doing? Are you male or female? Look at your feet first. What type of footwear or shoes are you wearing? Now move up the body and see exactly how you are clothed. How are you dressed? How old are you? What are you doing right now? What is happening around you? Are you outdoors or indoors? Is it day or night? Is it hot or cold? What country or land do you live in or are you from? Now focus on this one carefully—what do people call you? What is the year? Take a few moments; numbers may appear right in front of your awareness. You will be informed of exactly what year this is. Take a few more moments and let any additional information about the environment that you find yourself in as well as yourself crystallize and become clear in your awareness. Take a few moments. Let any additional information be made clear to you.

PLAY NEW AGE MUSIC FOR 3 MINUTES

Very good now. Listen very carefully to my voice now. Sleep now and rest. Detach yourself from this scene just for a moment. I'm going to be counting forward from 1 to 5. When I reach the count of 5, you're going to be moving forward to a significant event that will occur in this lifetime which will affect you personally. It will also most probably affect those close to you; it may involve your parents, friends, or people who are close to you in this lifetime. I want you to move forward to a significant event, but also a positive one. Focus carefully now. Sleep now and rest and listen now as I count forward from 1 to 5. On the count of 5 you will be moving forward in time to a significant positive event that is going to occur to you. 1, moving forward, slowly, carefully, comfortably. 2, feeling good as you move forward in time. 3, halfway there. 4, almost there, 5.

Now again focus on yourself and the environment you find yourself in. What are you doing now and why are you in this environment? Has anything changed since I last spoke with you? What is happening around you? Are there any other people around you who are important to you? Are they male or female? Are they friends or relatives? How do they relate to you? Why are they important to you? Focus on your clothes now, starting with your feet first. How are you dressed? Are you dressed any differently than when I last spoke with you? Move all the way up your body and perceive how you are dressed. Then look at the people next to you; are they dressed any differently? About how old are you now? Focus on that for a moment—a number will appear to you—about how old are you right now? Where exactly are you? Are you outdoors or indoors? Is it day or night? What season is this? What kind of occupation do you have? What do you do to pass the time? What do you do with your day? Focus on how you spend your time. Now I want you to focus on an event that's going to be happening right now that you find yourself right in the middle of. I want you to take this event right through to completion. I want you to spend a few moments and carry whatever this event is through to completion. This will be a positive or happy event only. Take a few moments and carry this event through to completion.

PLAY NEW AGE MUSIC FOR 3 MINUTES

All right now. Sleep now and rest. Detach yourself from this scene you are experiencing and listen to my voice again. You're going to be moving forward now by a period of a minimum of three years. It can be as long as necessary, but should be a minimum of three years. You will not have died or undergone any traumatic episode. It will be at least three years further in time. Now I want you to move forward to a significant event that is going to affect not only the kind of work that you do but also yourself personally. It will affect the way you relate to certain people—people who are close to you perhaps, or it will affect certain goals that you have. I want you to move forward to this very significant time which is going to be positive, neutral, or happy and it will be at least three years from now. On the count of 5, move forward very carefully and comfortably. 1, moving forward. 2, moving further forward. 3, halfway there. 4, almost there, 5. Now examine what you perceive around you. What has transpired since I last saw you? Focus on yourself first. Perceive where you are, how you are dressed, what environment you are in, where you are located if it was a different physical environment, and who you are with? Take a few moments and let this information crystallize and become clear into your awareness.

PLAY NEW AGE MUSIC FOR 3 MINUTES

All right now. Sleep now and rest. Detach yourself from this scene. We're going to be moving forward again on the count of 5. This time you're going to be moving forward to a scene that is going to signify or illustrate the maximum achievements that you accomplished in this lifetime, personally or professionally. You'll be surrounded by the people that affect you most in this lifetime. You will be achieving the maximum amount of success or goals, or whatever else you wanted to accomplish in this lifetime. Move forward to this maximum accomplishment in this lifetime on the count of 5. 1, moving forward slowly, carefully, comfortably. 2, moving further forward. 3, halfway there. 4, almost there, 5. Now, take a few moments and see where you find yourself. What is your environment? What has happened and why this time of your life is so important to you? Focus on it, see what you've accomplished, and let all the information be made clear to you.

PLAY NEW AGE MUSIC FOR 3 MINUTES

Now that you've been able to perceive this particular period of your life, I want you to be able to evaluate your life. I want you to find out what goals you were supposed to accomplish and what you actually did accomplish. What do you feel that you learned from this lifetime? What do you feel that you have gained from this lifetime—in your own personal goals, family life, relationships? Let the information flow. What did you gain? Now let's focus on what you weren't able to achieve. Focus on what you felt you would have liked more time for. What do you feel that you just weren't able to accomplish and why? Focus on that. Let the information flow. Now remember in this particular lifetime you are still alive. I want you now to focus on your activities, whatever you're involved in this particular scene to evaluate why this lifetime was important to you. What necessary or needed experience did you gain from this lifetime? Focus on this now. Let the information flow into your awareness.

PLAY NEW AGE MUSIC FOR 3 MINUTES

All right now. Sleep now and rest. You did very, very well. Listen verv carefully. I'm going to count forward now from 1 to 5, one more time. This time when I reach 5, you will be back in the present. You wil! be able to remember everything you experienced and re-experienced. You'll feel very relaxed and refreshed. You'll be able to do whatever you have planned for the rest of the day or evening. You'll feel very positive about what you've just experienced and very motivated about your confidence and ability to play this tape again to experience additional lifetimes. All right now. 1, very, very deep. 2, you're getting a little bit lighter. 3, you're getting much, much lighter. 4, very, very light. 5, awaken. Wide awake and refreshed.

SOULMATES

Love relationships are by far the most rewarding of all karmic entanglements. Couples quickly find out that they have been together before in many past lives. They will also be together again in future lifetimes. When there is a problem in a relationship, past regressions can often pinpoint the exact cause of the problem. One partner may have deserted his wife in a past life and thus incurred a karmic debt. In the life prior to that one the wife that was deserted may have deserted her husband, or perhaps she accidentally caused his death. Thus, a cycle of karmic debt and retribution was established. In relating to a significant other, there are two challenges. One is to understand oneself, and the other is to know the soul of the other. The better you get to know your significant other, the greater will be your understanding of yourself.

Before I begin describing cases of soulmates, a classification system needs to be mentioned. Since 1974 I have worked with over 11,000 patients. More than 33,000 past life regressions and future life progressions were conducted on this group of people. From these experiences I observed three totally separate kinds of soulmates.

The first type is what I call a *true soulmate*. This category consists of souls that have originated from the same oversoul at the exact same time. Others call this type the twin flame or twin soul. You and your true soulmate are from the same energy source and are perfectly compatible. My research has established that you will not encounter this soulmate until the very end of your karmic cycle. It is at this time that your soul's energy will be perfect and, assuming your counterpart has perfected him- or herself, you are eligible for this merging as you both—now one perfect soul— ascend to the higher planes (see Figure 4). If you were to meet your true soulmate prior to this it would spoil any other relationship. No other soul could possibly match your true soulmate's qualities.

Second, we have the *boundary soulmate*. This is a positive relationship, but you have known this soul only in a limited number of past lives. There are differences and some minor problems with this person (soul) but, all in all, it is a positive experience.

Last, we have the *retribution soulmate*. This is the only type that may be negative. You feel irresistibly drawn to this person but the results are almost always hard and traumatic. This soul has been in some of your past lives, usually exhibiting the same destructive pattern. If you have had both positive and negative relationships with a significant other in previous lives, this category could apply.

My experience suggests a "Miss or Mr. Right Now" effect, versus a permanent mate. This does not preclude the possibility that you can have a fulfilling life together with one person, but merely states that your growth, and that of your partner, is very likely to have a time limit. After that term ends, it is to both of your advantages (if you want to grow spiritually) to part and find another "soulmate" (ideally one functioning at a more evolved level).

The following script will help attract a soulmate into your life.

Now listen very carefully. I want you to imagine a bright white light coming down from above and entering the top of your head, filling your entire body. See it, feel it, and it becomes reality. Now imagine an aura of pure white light emanating from your heart region, again surrounding your entire body, protecting you. See it, feel it, and it becomes reality. Now only your higher self, masters and guides, and highly evolved loving entities who mean you well will be able to influence you during this or any other hypnotic session. You are totally protected by this aura of pure white light.

In a few moments, I am going to count from 1 to 20. As I do so, you will feel yourself rising up to the superconscious mind level where you will be able to receive information from your higher self and masters and guides. You will also be able to overview all of your past, present, and future lives. Number 1, rising up. 2, 3, 4, rising higher. 5, 6, 7, letting information flow. 8, 9, 10, you are halfway there. 11, 12, 13, feel yourself rising even higher. 14, 15, 16, almost there. 17, 18, 19, number 20, you are there. Take a moment and orient yourself to the superconscious mind level.

PLAY NEW AGE MUSIC FOR 1 MINUTE

You are now in a deep hypnotic trance. You are in complete control and able to access this limitless power of your superconscious mind. I want you to be open and flow with this experience. You are always protected by the white light.

Now I would like you to ask your higher self to assist you in attracting a soulmate into your life. Trust your higher self and your own ability to allow any thoughts, feelings, or impressions to come into your subconscious mind concerning this goal. Do this now.

PLAY NEW AGE MUSIC FOR 3 MINUTES

Focus on the kind of man or woman that you want in your life. If you could have precisely the kind of person you want for a special love relationship, what would he or she be like? What would be his or her qualifications? This is someone very compatible with you. This is someone that meshes with your primary values, your major goals, and your direction in life.

This is someone who fits in with your other primary relationships and adds to them. This is someone that you get along with, can live with, and feel empowered by. This is someone who is a good, healthy choice for you. This is someone you love, admire, respect, and trust, and who feels the same about you. This someone is your own best friend, companion, lover, and partner, all in one—a mutual admiration society, in which caring about one another and commitment to the relationship grows day by day.

This soul is one with whom you shared only positive past lives. This mate will assist you, and you will assist him or her in raising your respective soul's energy. See this person in front of you. Take them by the hand and embrace them. Do this now.

PLAY NEW AGE MUSIC FOR 4 MINUTES

You have done very well. Now I want you to further open up the channels of communication by removing any obstacles and allowing yourself to receive information and experiences that will directly apply to and help better your present lifetime. Allow yourself to receive more advanced and more specific information from your higher self and masters and guides to raise your frequency and improve your karmic subcycle. Do this now.

PLAY NEW AGE MUSIC FOR 4 MINUTES

All right now. Sleep now and rest. You did very, very well. Listen very carefully. When I reach the count of 5, you will be back in the present. You will be able to remember everything that you experienced and re-experienced. You'll feel very relaxed, refreshed and you'll be able to do whatever you have planned for the rest of the day or evening. You'll feel very positive about your confidence and ability to play this tape again to experience your higher self. All right now. 1, very, very deep. 2, you're getting a little bit lighter. 3, you're getting much lighter. 4, very, very light. 5, awaken. Wide awake and refreshed.

Carl came to see me several years ago. He was bothered by what is referred to as secondary impotency. This means that Carl is able to function sexually at some times, but is not at other times. Physiologically, there was nothing wrong with Carl, but psychologically he had problems.

Carl described three past lives with his current wife Martha. During the Middle Ages, he was a soldier named Hans, serving in a German castle. Hans had wanted to take over this castle ever since the lord of the castle died. The lord's widow (Martha) had no plans to move. Hans organized a rebellion in the army, but the lord's wife amassed her own troops and put down this rebellion. Hans swore to get back at Martha just before he was killed.

In France about 300 years later Carl reincarnated as Ladin, a fisherman married to Jeanne (Martha). Jeanne died while giving birth to their son. Ladin stated quite clearly, "I'll never go through that again."

Their third lifetime together was quite different. Both Carl and Martha were male and living in Maine in the early 1800s. One day Carl accidentally shot his best friend Sam (Martha) while hunting. Carl wasn't able to find a physician until it was too late. Sam said, "Don't touch me," when Carl finally arrived with the doctor, making Carl feel guilty and useless. Carl's subconscious mind remembered this and his present impotency was a direct result of this incident.

This case illustrates changing sexes between lives. Martha was a male in her last life as Sam. Although most of your lives will be lived as one sex, the karmic cycle requires that you experience lives as both sexes.

When Carl was Ladin in eighteenth-century France, he blamed himself for Martha's (Jeanne's) death. She died in labor and Carl promised himself that he wouldn't go through that experience again. He didn't want to have any more children. In his next life as the hunter in Maine, he would not marry again. One might say that he indirectly caused the death of Martha as Ladin, but as the hunter he directly caused Martha's (Sam's) death by accidentally shooting him. The amount of guilt that Carl brought with him from these past lives was enormous.

In the lifetime as Hans, Carl forced Martha out of the castle. Martha won in the end and caused Carl's death. Carl sought karmic retribution indirectly during his next two lives as Ladin and the hunter. His present life might have ended the same way. Fortunately, Carl was able to see the causes of his sexual difficulties.

It doesn't matter who initiated the problem. All that really matters is that the problems get resolved. Today Martha and Carl have no sexual problems. They love each other very much and have finally learned to live together in peace. It takes many lifetimes for most couples to finally resolve their difficulties.

My most dynamic case of a retribution soulmate relationship is reported in my book *The Search for Grace: The True Story of Murder and Reincarnation*.[1] The patient, whom I call Ivy, was obsessively attracted to John. John literally tried to murder Ivy on three separate occasions, but Ivy was unable to break away from this relationship. The soul of John had murdered Ivy in twenty of the forty-six past lives that Ivy and I uncovered through hypnosis.

Ivy wanted desperately to break off the relationship and end the recurrent nightmares from which she awoke screaming in terror,

---

1 St. Paul: Llewellyn Publications, 1997.

murdered over and over by the same mysterious man—but she just couldn't seem to pull herself free.

Ivy lived in Buffalo, New York, in the 1920s as a woman named Grace Doze. She was a cold and calculating woman who had little respect and much dislike for her husband, Chester. Grace had many affairs during her marriage—she was a real Roaring Twenties party girl. She was responsible enough not to abandon her son, Cliff, but beyond that her lifestyle was hedonistic.[2]

One evening in early May of 1927, Grace met a bootlegger named Jake at a speakeasy. They saw quite a bit of each other during the next two weeks. She decided to leave Chester and move in with Jake immediately following her regular Tuesday night swimming session on May 17 at the local high school.

Jake was drunk when he picked up Grace on that fateful evening at about 9:45 P.M. When Grace mentioned that her son Cliff would be living with them, Jake became abusive. He was quick to anger even when he wasn't drinking, and during the drive their discussion rapidly escalated into a heated argument. Without warning, Jake punched Grace with his right hand. She was conscious, but in pain. Jake then strangled her until she died.

I have to wonder if the subconscious force that motivated Ivy so strongly to want to be regressed into this life had to do with the deep synchronicity that brought us together, and brought her story through me to CBS, and thus to the public at large. She gave me over two dozen facts that were verified by an independent researcher. Perhaps Grace Doze's unhappy spirit could not rest without clearing up the mystery of her death. Now Ivy was finally able to break this karmic bond and go on with her life.

There is a tendency in life to create your own reality. In fact, quantum physics mathematically establishes this. The energy you receive from others is a function of the energy you yourself send out. "What goes around comes around." Relationships can be

---

2 CBS aired this case as a television movie on May 17, 1994, sixty-seven years to the hour after Grace Doze died.

quite karmic, with origins going back thousands of years. The next time you are introduced to someone who affects you extremely, ask them, "Didn't we meet in a past life?"

REGRESSION CASES

The cases that follow also involve regression back into previous lifetimes. I have arranged these examples into categories reflecting the various pathologies reported by the patients. In each case I will give a superconscious mind tap ("cleansing") script demonstrating how this issue can be resolved.

Fear of Dentists

Due to negative conditioning, patients frequently are terrified to have dental work performed. A prior traumatic experience with a dentist as a child leaves a lasting negative impression in the subconscious mind. This impression may affect the patient's attitude toward oral health care for the rest of their life.

Now listen very carefully. I want you to imagine a bright white light coming down from above and entering the top of your head, filling your entire body. See it, feel it and it becomes reality. Now imagine an aura of pure white light emanating from your heart region, again surrounding your entire body, protecting you. See it, feel it, and it becomes reality. Now only your higher self, masters and guides, and highly evolved loving entities who mean you well will be able to influence you during this or any other hypnotic session. You are totally protected by this aura of pure white light.

In a few moments, I am going to count from 1 to 20. As I do so you will feel yourself rising up to the superconscious mind level where you will be able to receive information from your higher self and masters and guides. You will also be able to overview all of your past, present, and future lives. Number 1, rising up. 2, 3, 4, rising higher. 5, 6, 7, letting information flow. 8, 9, 10, you are halfway there. 11, 12, 13, feel yourself rising even higher. 14, 15, 16, almost there. 17, 18, 19, number 20. Now you are there. Take a moment and orient yourself to the superconscious mind level.

PLAY NEW AGE MUSIC FOR 1 MINUTE

You are now in a deep hypnotic trance and from this superconscious mind level, there exists a complete understanding and resolution of the fear of dentists. You are in complete control and able to access the limitless power of your superconscious mind. I want you to be open and flow with this experience. You are always protected by the white light.

Now ask your higher self to explore the origin of your dental fear. Trust your higher self and your own ability to bring thoughts, feelings, or impressions into your subconscious mind concerning this goal. Do this now.

PLAY NEW AGE MUSIC FOR 3 MINUTES

Now I would like you to let go of the situation, regardless of how simple or complicated it may seem. At this time I want you to visualize yourself in your current life and consciousness free of this issue.

When you are seated in the dental chair you will think of the number 20 three times in succession and immediately feel the relaxation developing. The dental chair will feel very soft and comfortable and will remind you of your favorite chair at home. Concentrate on enjoying this wonderful, relaxing feeling. The various sounds that you will hear will have the same soothing effect as listening to your favorite music.

Your fears for a dental appointment will cease to exist. You will be able to allow the necessary dental treatment to be carried out. You will experience no fear whatsoever during the entire time you spend with the dentist. You will experience no fear whatsoever during appointments in which teeth have to be removed, filled, etc. You are steadily losing your desires to be afraid of a dentist or dental procedures.

During all your dental procedures, you will be relaxed, calm, comfortable, and you will experience a normal gag reflex. Any excessive gag reflex will be eliminated and you will remain relaxed, calm, and comfortable during the dental procedure.

PLAY NEW AGE MUSIC FOR 4 MINUTES

You have done very well. Now I want you to further open up the channels of communications by removing any obstacles and allowing yourself to receive information and experiences that will directly apply to and help better your present lifetime. Allow yourself to receive more advanced and more specific information from your higher self and masters and guides to raise your frequency and improve your karmic subcycle. Do this now.

PLAY NEW AGE MUSIC FOR 4 MINUTES

■
■
■
■
■
■
■
■
■
■
All right now. Sleep now and rest. You did very, very well. Listen very carefully. I'm going to count forward now from 1 to 5. When I reach the count of 5 you will be back in the present, you will be able to remember everything you experienced and re-experienced. You'll feel very relaxed, refreshed, and you'll be able to do whatever you have planned for the rest of the day or evening. You'll feel very positive about what you've experienced and very motivated about your confidence and ability to play this tape again, to experience your higher self...All right now. 1, very, very deep. 2, you're getting a little bit lighter. 3, you're getting much, much lighter. 4, very, very light. 5, awaken. Wide awake and refreshed.

This case study concerns a fifty-one-year-old housewife who was fearful of dentists. Miriam called my office in September 1978, stating she had not been to the dentist in over ten years and knew she had many dental problems. Her dental fear was related to other problems in her life; she had a low opinion of herself and felt that if she could somehow eliminate this phobia, her relationships with her husband, children, and friends would also improve.

During her first appointment we discussed her dental history; she could not remember a traumatic incident involving prior dental treatment. She hoped to learn through hypnosis why she had developed the dental phobia and to eliminate this fear permanently.

The possibility of a past life cause was explained to Miriam. Miriam seemed quite interested in my explanation of karma and reincarnation, and although skeptical, she seemed to trust me and was willing to try almost anything to get to the cause of her phobia. I gave her a past life regression conditioning tape and made an appointment for a few weeks later. Miriam seemed excited when she entered the office that fall afternoon and, as usual, she went quickly into a deeply relaxed trance.

Miriam is a very soft-spoken woman, and in the four weeks that I had known her prior to this regression, she had never used any form of foul language. Now her voice dropped in pitch and her language became coarse. During most of this session she held her right cheek as if she were in severe pain, although consciously no such discomfort existed.

Miriam reported that she lived in a small town in Kansas in 1838. There were no dentists in her area, so she had to go to the local blacksmith, Smitty, for an extraction. There was a physician in town, but he did not perform any dentistry. It was not uncommon for blacksmiths and barbers to do dentistry at that time.

I progressed Anna forward a few hours. She had gone into the saloon and consumed many glasses of whiskey to premedicate herself. We discovered that her husband had died a few years earlier and she ran their small farm with the help of two hired hands. Anna was a very strong and resourceful woman in this life and had many friends. The only problem area of her life was her teeth. Smitty had removed seven or eight teeth from her over the years and every time he extracted one, Anna went through pure hell.

Since there was no anesthesia at this time, all dentistry, usually consisting of extractions, was performed while physically restraining the patient. Here is a portion of the transcript of this session.

Dr. G.:   What is happening now?

Miriam: Smitty is standing over me now with the pliers in his hand. (Her voice was very shaky again.)

Dr. G.:   Where is Paul?

Miriam: He is behind me, holding my head back.

Dr. G.:   Continue on, Anna.

Miriam: Smitty puts those damn pliers in my mouth. I can taste the rust on them. (She grimaced and held on very tightly to the arms of my recliner.)

Dr. G.:   What happened next?

Miriam: He puts the pliers on my back tooth. It hurts so bad now. The whiskey isn't working.

Dr. G.:   Go on, Anna.

Miriam: He yanks real hard and I try to turn my head, but I can't. That Paul is so strong. (Her knuckles were beginning to turn white because she was holding onto my chair so tightly.) My tooth! Yeoow! Yeoow! Yeoow!

Anna screamed so loudly it startled me, but she calmed down quickly and sank back in the chair, exhausted. She rested for about five minutes and then we resumed the questioning.

Dr. G.:   Anna, are you all right?

Miriam: Oh yes, I'm fine now. That Smitty is okay. He got that damned tooth with one yank. (She is relieved now.)

Dr. G.:   Does your jaw hurt?

Miriam: No, not now. I'll be okay, I'm bleeding, but I know it won't be long before that stops.

Dr. G.:   What are you going to do now?

Miriam: I'm going back to the saloon and get me some more whiskey. Then I'll go home and try to forget about today.

I progressed Anna throughout this day and the next day. Surprisingly, she didn't develop an infection from the dirty pliers. Her resistance to disease was good. Anna was able to work on her farm the following day. She was quite a remarkable woman.

Miriam seemed to admire Anna and her qualities of strength, assertiveness, frankness, and honesty. After this session, I discussed my observations with Miriam. Miriam agreed that she found Anna a most unusual and admirable woman. Anna's self-confidence and ability to get along with people represented quite a contrast to Miriam.

Miriam was skeptical about whether she had actually lived before as Anna, but she decided that she would return to me for much-needed dental treatment. During that treatment, a number of teeth were restored, two root canals were filled, and five additional teeth were crowned. Miriam showed very little apprehension throughout the entire treatment and was an excellent patient. Of more interest were the other improvements in her life. Miriam was quickly becoming more self-confident and assertive. She reported to me a closer relationship with her husband and her children. Her friends and relatives also noted this behavioral change. Some asked her if she was taking some medication, and others asked her if she was seeing a psychiatrist. Miriam reported feeling like a different woman.

We may take credit for her dental improvement, but it was a combination of Miriam's understanding and past life regression therapy that resulted in the other changes.

Depression

Debbie came to see me to be treated for depression more than ten years ago. This mood disorder began shortly after she started dating Mark, an older man. Mark felt their relationship seemed to fit into an established pattern from the beginning. "We stayed in it comfortably and it seemed like we had been in it for years," Debbie said.

As certain events transpired, Debbie seemed to turn inward. "A couple of Saturdays ago, nothing was going right," Debbie said. "It turned out Mark had fallen and hurt his leg. I kept telling my mother, 'Something feels wrong today.' It's really awful. It's strange, but Mark and I, we seem to have that kind of tie."

Debbie said, "Our personalities felt so compatible. We felt that we had been through this before, yet we never discussed it. Once he kidded me, 'Maybe we did love before. Maybe there is no other explanation.' I've never felt this way with anyone else." In her past life, she was a psychic named Aya, living in Athens in 50 B.C. A Roman politician named Marcus convinced her to live with him in Rome. Because she broke her vow of celibacy, she lost much of her psychic ability, and was prevented from reaching her full potential.

I surmised that by reliving her Grecian life—a lot of this life was spent in Rome with Marcus—she was able to understand why she was attracted to her boyfriend in this life (Mark). He is the reincarnation of Marcus.

By recognizing that Mark was the Roman politician of her past life, Debbie was able to discern that, their good relationship notwithstanding, it had still resulted in the earlier loss of her psychic abilities and had imposed severe limits on her ability to live up to her potential. In this life, had Mark maintained another relationship with her, Debbie night have been tremendously limited in her personal and professional growth.

After her hypnotherapy, Debbie overcame her depressions. She realized that she wasn't supposed to be with her old love because it would have limited her. She is now quite an independent person and very career-oriented. Her goal is not to be the typical American housewife.

After I regressed Debbie past her death as Aya, I asked her what she had learned. She replied, "I no longer need to be with Marcus. The dark cloud lifted. I can now go on."

Debbie reflected, "Maybe Mark is presenting a lesson I have yet to learn. Maybe this particular life is presenting the same situation again and I have to choose again, because I am tending to go the same way." She later terminated her relationship with Mark.

"I have had certain psychic things happen to me that are totally unexplained. Dreams that come to me, feelings that I've been somewhere before," Debbie said.

Even so, she felt that reliving her past life not only "liberated" her, it also explained the origin of her psychic abilities.

In an altogether different vein, Yvonne's depression was a low-grade condition, but it had persisted for many years. She was also a compulsive eater. Her depression usually set in when she was alone in her apartment; her husband worked longer hours than she.

During World War II, she had been a twenty-year-old seamstress in Germany. In that past life, she took a trip to visit relatives. When she returned, she found that all of her family had been killed by the Nazis. She starved herself to death to join them. Yvonne just couldn't bear the thought of being alone in that lifetime. This self-defeating pattern manifested itself in her current lifetime.

Now listen very carefully. I want you to imagine a bright white light coming down from above and entering the top of your head, filling your entire body. See it, feel it, and it becomes reality. Now imagine an aura of pure white light emanating from your heart region, again surrounding your entire body, protecting you. See it, feel it, and it becomes reality. Now only your higher self, masters and guides, and highly evolved loving entities who mean you well will be able to influence you during this or any other hypnotic session. You are totally protected by this aura of pure white light.

In a few moments I am going to count from 1 to 20. As I do so you will feel yourself rising up to the superconscious mind level, where you will receive information from your higher self and masters and guides. You will also be able to overview your past, present, and future lives. Number 1, rising up. 2, 3, 4, rising higher. 5, 6, 7, letting information flow. 8, 9, 10, you are halfway there. 11, 12, 13, feel yourself rising even higher. 14, 15, 16, almost there. 17, 18, 19, number 20, you are there. Take a moment and orient yourself to the superconscious mind level.

PLAY NEW AGE MUSIC FOR 1 MINUTE

You are now in a deep hypnotic trance and from this superconscious mind level, there exists a complete understanding and resolution of the fear of the depression. You are in complete control and able to access this limitless power of your superconscious mind. I want you to be open and flow with this experience. You are always protected by the white light.

Now I would like you to ask your higher self to explore the origin of your depression. Trust your higher self to explore the origin of your depression. Trust your higher self and your own ability to allow any thoughts, feelings, or impressions concerning this goal to come into your subconscious mind. Do this now.

PLAY NEW AGE MUSIC FOR 3 MINUTES

Now I would like you to let go of the situation, regardless of how simple or complicated it may seem. At this time I want you to visualize yourself in your current life and consciousness free of this issue. Perceive yourself in your daily life with more energy and confidence. Mentally create your new reality, free of depression as you relate to your family, friends, work environment, and your local community.

PLAY NEW AGE MUSIC FOR 4 MINUTES

You have done very well. Now I want you to further open up the channels of communication by removing any obstacles and allowing yourself to receive information and experiences that will directly apply to and help better your present lifetime. Allow yourself to receive more advanced and more specific information from your higher self and masters and guides, to raise your frequency and improve your karmic subcycle. Do this now.

PLAY NEW AGE MUSIC FOR 4 MINUTES

You have done very well. Now I want you to further open up the channels of communication by removing any obstacles and allowing yourself to receive information and experiences that will directly apply and to help better your present lifetime. Allow yourself to receive more advanced and more specific information from your higher self and masters and guides, to raise your frequency and improve your karmic subcycle. Do this now.

PLAY NEW AGE MUSIC FOR 4 MINUTES

All right now. Sleep now and rest. You did very, very well. Listen very carefully. I'm going to count forward now from 1 to 5. When I reach the count of 5, you will be back in the present. You will be able to remember everything you experienced and re-experienced. You'll feel very relaxed, refreshed, and you'll be able to do whatever you have planned for the rest of the day or evening. You'll feel very positive about what you've just experienced and very motivated about your confidence and ability to play this tape again to experience your higher self. All right now. 1, very, very deep. 2, you're getting a little bit lighter. 3, you're getting much, much lighter. 4, very, very light. 5, awaken. Wide awake and refreshed.

Hypnosis to Stop Smoking

A forty-three-year-old male builder came to me to help him quit smoking. Since smoking is a response to stress, we traced back the origins of his stress and his underlying desire for self-punishment.

David, in an eighteenth-century life as a shepherd, was frustrated in his attempt to go after a group of thieves. These thieves raided David's flock of sheep, killed some of the shepherds, and burned a number of the tribe's tents. As a nomad, David experienced stress and frustration. A council of elders ruled David's tribe; they made all of the decisions concerning the tribe's actions.

These elders felt that pursuing the murderers would leave the flocks, the women, and the children defenseless. As fate would have it, the elders were soon proven correct. A second attack by another gang of rustlers was fortunately repelled by David's tribe. Had they left the camp unguarded in order to capture the first band of marauders, a complete disaster would have resulted.

During the Middle Ages this patient was a priest in India named Bevar. Bevar was a scholarly, dedicated priest with a true concern for people. Unfortunately, the head priest, Navu, didn't share Bevar's attitude. Navu was very greedy, increasing the tax burden on the already impoverished townspeople, many of whom were starving. Bevar sought to return some of the temple's money to the people, but Navu objected, frustrating Bevar's attempts. Bevar became angry but couldn't express his emotions. Navu eventually died and Bevar collected funds for the poor.

In both lives, stress was involved and the patient encountered serious obstructions. Navu would not let Bevar do what he wanted. Like David the shepherd, Bevar was frustrated; the tension was rising. Note also that Bevar had to submit to the orders of an authority figure, a situation that David could relate to.

One additional past life was uncovered, one that helped this patient to permanently eliminate his tobacco addiction. He described several nineteenth-century scenes where he murdered various people. He was a member of a band of orphans, all of whom were in their early twenties. He was a Jewish youth disguised in Arab garb. He and his band would drift from town to town, murdering Arabs. Apparently Arabs had killed his parents, and those of the other youths in the gang. These youths were hellbent on finding the men responsible for murdering their parents.

When they became frustrated by the fruitlessness of their vengeful search, these youths indiscriminately opened fire on any Arab they saw. These attacks had been going on for over two years. Eventually, the youths were able to avenge their parents' deaths by killing those responsible, but this did not end the band's thirst for Arab blood, and their killing raids continued.

Finally, the gang was butchered in an ambush and the youth with them. He was on a real vengeance trip in that life, venting his frustrations with abandon. Today he is about the least vengeful person I have ever met.

I compared many of his present experiences with those of his three past lives. In all three of his lives, he was frustrated. As David, he had violent thoughts but never acted on them. As the Jewish band leader, he acted on these urges. He is presently a builder. He waits for money and projects to come in. He might have to deal with bad weather, labor problems, construction delays, and bureaucratic red tape. Most of the pressures driving him to smoke were from his business. He no longer smokes.

Now listen very carefully. I want you to imagine a bright white light coming down from above and entering the top of your head, filling your entire body. See it, feel it, and it becomes reality. Now imagine an aura of pure white light emanating from your heart region, again surrounding your entire body, protecting you. See it, feel it, and it becomes reality. Now only your higher self, masters and guides, and highly evolved loving entities who mean you well will be able to influence you during this or any other hypnotic session. You are totally protected by this aura of pure white light.

In a few moments, I am going to count from 1 to 20. As I do so you will feel yourself rising up to the superconscious mind level, where you will receive information from your higher self and masters and guides. You will also overview your past, present and future lives. Number 1, rising up. 2, 3, 4, rising higher. 5, 6, 7, letting information flow. 8, 9, 10, you are halfway there. 11, 12, 13, feel yourself rising even higher. 14, 15, 16, almost there. 17, 18, 19, number 20, you are there. Take a moment and orient yourself to the superconscious mind level.

PLAY NEW AGE MUSIC FOR 1 MINUTE

You are now in a deep hypnotic trance, and from this superconscious mind level, there exists a complete understanding and resolution of the smoking habit. You are in complete control and able to access this limitless power of you, superconscious mind. I want you to be open and flow with this experience. You are always protected by the white light.

At this time, I would like to ask your higher self to explore the origin of your smoking habit. Trust your higher self and your own ability to allow any thoughts, feelings, or impressions concerning this goal to come into your subconscious mind. Do this now.

PLAY NEW AGE MUSIC FOR 3 MINUTES

Now I would like you to let go of the situation, regardless of how simple or complicated it may seem. At this time I want you to visualize yourself in your current life and consciousness free of this issue.

Take a moment now and imagine yourself driving on a road and arriving at a fork on this road. The left fork is a clean, newly paved, unobstructed road leading to a brand new highway. It is labeled for non-smokers. The right fork is a rocky, obstructed road and leads to a dead end. It is labeled for smokers. You choose which one you want to take.

PLAY NEW AGE MUSIC FOR 4 MINUTES

You have done very well. Now I want you to further open up the channels of communication by removing any obstacles and allowing yourself to receive information and experiences that will directly apply to and help better your present lifetime. Allow yourself to receive more advanced and more specific information from your higher self and masters and guides to raise your frequency and improve your karmic subcycle. Do this now.

PLAY NEW AGE MUSIC FOR 4 MINUTES

All right now. Sleep now and rest. You did very, very well. Listen very carefully. I'm going to count forward now from 1 to 5. When I reach the count of 5, you will be back in the present, and you will be able to remember everything you experienced and reexperienced. You'll feel very relaxed, refreshed, and you'll be able to do whatever you have planned for

- the rest of the day or evening. You'll feel very positive
- about what you've just experienced and very moti-
- vated about your confidence and ability to play this
- tape again to experience your higher self. All right
  now. 1, very, very deep. 2, you're getting a little bit
  lighter. 3, you're getting much, much lighter. 4, very,
  very light. 5. awaken. Wide awake and refreshed.

Overeating

Elaine was obese. She was five feet three inches tall and weighed 175 pounds when she came to my office in 1993. As a dental hygienist, she was well trained in nutrition and knew better than to engage in immoderate eating.

Another problem affecting Elaine concerned her relationships with men. She simply didn't trust men, having invited quite a few "Mr. Wrongs" into her life.

The western United States during the early 1800s was the setting of her past life. She lived in a small cabin in the woods with her husband. They were married only a few months when a group of escaped convicts murdered her husband and raped her.

These desperados used her cabin as a hideout for several years, keeping Elaine prisoner and continually abusing her. One day, they decided to leave, complaining that she was getting old and they wanted someone younger. Elaine died of starvation shortly after their departure. She wasted away, having lost the will to live.

The karmic carryover of starvation manifested itself as a desire to overcompensate in this present life with excess food consumption. After applying cleansing techniques, at a two-year follow-up Elaine now weighs 125 pounds and is engaged to a man she loves, and who appears to love her.

A fifty-three-year-old widowed female realtor came to see me for help in losing weight. In a past life in Switzerland in the 1700s, she was a very attractive female. However, she had three sisters who were very obese, and they tried to force my patient to overeat. When she refused, one of her sisters tried to kill her. Her father saved her, but her life remained in constant danger. She finally gave in and became obese. The man she loved abandoned her for another woman. Her sisters in that life are her sisters in this life. The man she loved but lost was her husband (now deceased) in this life.

Now listen very carefully. I want you to imagine a bright white light, coming down from above and entering the top of your head, filling your entire body. See it, feel it, and it becomes reality. Now imagine an aura of pure white light emanating from your heart region, again surrounding your entire body, protecting you. See it, feel it, and it becomes a reality. Now only your higher self, masters and guides, and highly evolved loving entities who mean you well will be able to influence you during this or any other hypnotic session. You are totally protected by this aura of pure white light.

In a few moments, I am going to count from 1 to 20. As I do so, you will feel yourself rising up to the superconscious mind level where you will receive information from your higher self and masters and guides. You will also be able to overview all of the past, present, and future lives. Number 1, rising up. 2, 3, 4, rising higher. 5, 6, 7, letting information flow. 8, 9, 10, you are halfway there. 11, 12, 13, feel yourself rising even higher. 14, 15, 16, almost there. 17, 18, 19, number 20, you are there. Take a moment and orient yourself to the superconscious mind level.

PLAY NEW AGE MUSIC FOR 1 MINUTE

You are now in a deep hypnotic trance, and from this superconscious mind level, there exists a complete understanding and resolution of the overeating problem. You are in complete control and able to access this limitless power of your superconscious mind. I want you to be open and flow with this experience. You are always protected by the white light.

At this time, ask your higher self to explore the origin of your tendency to overeat. Trust your higher self and your own ability to allow any thoughts, feelings, or impressions to come into your subconscious mind concerning this goal. Do this now.

PLAY NEW AGE MUSIC FOR 3 MINUTES

Now I would like you to let go of the situation, regardless of how simple or complicated it may seem. At this time I want you to visualize yourself in your current life and consciousness, free of this issue.

Imagine yourself being at your ideal weight. See a friend or mate shopping with you. He or she is amazed at your thin appearance. Now visualize two tables in front of you. The table on the right has all the foods you like that add unwanted weight (list examples). Now draw a large red X through the table and imagine yourself looking at yourself in a mirror (one that makes you appear very wide and short as in a carnival mirror).

The table on the left contains food that is healthy for you and that will not add unwanted weight—fish, eggs, lean meat, etc. Now draw a large yellow check through the table and imagine looking at yourself in

- a mirror (one that makes you appear tall and thin). Mentally tell yourself that you desire only the foods on the check-marked table. Imagine your friends and family telling you how great you look by (specify a date) weighing only ___ pounds.

- Visualize a photograph of yourself at your ideal weight. Visualize a photograph of yourself at your present weight. Now focus on the photograph of yourself at your ideal weight. The other photograph disappears. Imagine how it will feel at your ideal weight to bend over to tie your shoelace, walk, jog, and wear a bathing suit on the beach.

- Now, mentally select an ideal diet that will help you reach your ideal weight. Tell yourself that this is all the food your body will need or desire and it will not send hunger pangs for more.

PLAY NEW AGE MUSIC FOR 4 MINUTES

- You have done very well. Now I want you to further open up the channels of communication by removing any obstacles and allowing yourself to receive information and experiences that will directly apply to and help better your present lifetime. Allow yourself to receive more advanced and more specific information from your higher self and masters and guides to raise your frequency and improve your karmic subcycle. Do this now.

PLAY NEW AGE MUSIC FOR 4 MINUTES

- All right now. Sleep and rest. You did very well. Listen very carefully. I'm going to count forward now from 1 to 5. When I reach the count of 5 you will be back in the present, and you will be able to remember everything you experienced and re-experienced. You'll feel very relaxed, refreshed, and you'll be able to do whatever you have planned for the rest of the day or evening. You'll feel positive about what you've just experienced and very motivated about your confidence and ability to play this tape again to experience your higher self. All right now. 1, very, very deep. 2, you're getting a little lighter. 3, you're much, much lighter. 4, very, very light. 5, awaken. Wide awake and refreshed."

Overcoming Shyness

A twenty-eight-year-old female accountant came to me to help her overcome a shyness problem.

In a past life in Germany in the 1890s, my patient was a retarded male child locked up in an institution. He was mute and suffered chronic mistreatment at the hands of the other patients. Over the years, he became more and more frustrated and fearful of people.

He couldn't even complain about this abuse because he could not speak. At the age of sixteen, he finally committed suicide.

In another life in ancient Rome, she was stoned to death for being unjustly accused of adultery.

Now listen very carefully. I want you to imagine a bright white light, coming down from above and entering the top of your head, filling your entire body. See it, feel it, and it becomes reality. Now imagine an aura of pure white light emanating from your heart region, again surrounding your entire body, protecting you. See it, feel it, and it becomes a reality. Now only your higher self, masters and guides, and highly evolved loving entities who mean you well will be able to influence you during this or any other hypnotic session. You are totally protected by this aura of pure white light.

In a few moments, I am going to count from 1 to 20. As I do so you will feel yourself rising up to the superconscious mind level where you will be able to receive information from your higher self and masters and guides. You will also be able to overview all of the past, present, and future lives. Number 1, rising up. 2, 3, 4, rising higher. 5, 6, 7, letting information flow. 8, 9, 10, you are halfway there. 11, 12, 13, feel yourself rising even higher. 14, 15, 16, almost there. 17, 18, 19, number 20, you are there. Take a moment and orient yourself to the superconscious mind level

PLAY NEW AGE MUSIC FOR 1 MINUTE

You are now in a deep hypnotic trance, and from this superconscious mind level, there exists a complete understanding and resolution of the shyness issue. You are in complete control and able to access this limitless power of your superconscious mind. I want you to be open and flow with this experience. You are always protected by the white light.

At this time, I would like you to ask your higher self to explore the origin of your shyness. Trust your higher self and your own ability to allow any thoughts, feelings, or impressions to come into your subconscious mind concerning this goal. Do this now.

- PLAY NEW AGE MUSIC FOR 3 MINUTES

Now I would like you to let go of the situation, regardless of how simple or complicated it may seem. At this time I want you to visualize yourself in your daily life becoming more outgoing and confident about everything you do and say.

Every day...your nerves will become stronger and steadier. You will become so deeply interested in whatever you are doing...so deeply interested in whatever is going on...that your mind will become much less preoccupied with yourself...and you will become much less conscious of yourself...and your own feelings.

Every day...your mind will become much calmer and clearer...more composed...more placid...more tranquil. You will become much less easily worried...much less easily agitated...much less fearful and apprehensive...much less easily upset.

You will be able to think more clearly...you will be able to concentrate more easily...your memory will improve...and you will be able to see things in their true perspective...without magnifying them...without allowing them to get out of proportion.

Every day...you will become emotionally much calmer...much more settled...much less easily disturbed. And every day...you will experience a greater feeling of personal well-being...a greater feeling of personal safety and security...than you have felt for a long, long time. Every day...you will become...and you will remain...more and more completely relaxed...both mentally and physically.

And as you become...and as you remain...more relaxed...and less tense each day...so you will develop much more confidence in yourself...much more confidence in your ability to do so...not only what you have to do each day...but also...much more confidence in your ability to do whatever you ought to be able to do...without fear of failure...without fear of consequences...without anxiety...without uneasiness. Because of this...every day...you will feel more and more independent...more able to "stick up for yourself"...to stand upon your own two feet...to hold your own no matter how difficult or trying things may be.

Every day, in every way, you are getting better, better and better...negative thoughts and negative suggestions have no influence over you at any mind level.

And, because all these things will happen...exactly as I tell you they will happen...you are going to feel much happier...much more contented...much more cheerful...much more optimistic...much less easily discouraged...much less easily bothered.

PLAY NEW AGE MUSIC FOR 4 MINUTES

You have done very well. Now I want you to further open up the channels of communication by removing any obstacles and allowing yourself to receive information and experiences that will directly apply to and help better your present lifetime. Allow yourself to receive more advanced and more specific

- information from your higher self and masters and
- guides to raise your frequency and improve your
- karmic subcycle. Do this now.

- PLAY NEW AGE MUSIC FOR 4 MINUTES

- All right now. Sleep and rest. You did very well. Listen
- very carefully. I'm going to count forward now from
- 1 to 5. When I reach the count of 5 you will be back
- in the present, you will be able to remember every-
- thing you experienced and re-experienced. You'll feel
- very relaxed, refreshed, and you'll be able to do what-
- ever you have planned for the rest of the day or
- evening. You'll feel positive about what you've just
- experienced and motivated about your confidence
- and ability to again experience your higher self. All
- right now. 1, very, very deep. 2, you're getting a little
  lighter. 3, you're much, much lighter. 4, very, very
  light. 5, awaken. Wide awake and refreshed.

Fear of Abandonment

A thirty-one-year-old female nurse came to me to help her overcome an oppressive fear of abandonment pervading all her relationships with men. In a past life in Philadelphia in the 1890s, she
had been involved for years with a married man. One day he very
coldly broke off the relationship. She felt betrayed, hurt, abandoned, and ultimately drowned herself.

Now listen very carefully. I want you to imagine a
bright white light, coming down from above and
- entering the top of your head, filling your entire
- body. See it, feel it and it becomes reality. Now imag-
- ine an aura of pure white light emanating from your
  heart region, again surrounding your entire body,

protecting you. See it, feel it and it becomes a reality. Now only your higher self, masters and guides, and highly evolved loving entities who mean you well will be able to influence you during this or any other hypnotic session. You are totally protected by this aura of pure white light.

In a few moments, I am going to count from 1 to 20. As I do so you will feel yourself rising up to the superconscious mind level where you will receive information from your higher self and masters and guides. You will also overview all of the past, present, and future lives. Number 1, rising up. 2, 3, 4, rising higher. 5, 6, 7, letting information flow. 8, 9, 10, you are halfway there. 11, 12, 13, feel yourself rising even higher. 14, 15, 16, almost there. 17, 18, 19, number 20, you are there. Take a moment and orient yourself to the superconscious mind level.

PLAY NEW AGE MUSIC FOR 1 MINUTE

You are now in a deep hypnotic trance and from this superconscious mind level, there exists a complete understanding and resolution of the fear of abandonment. You are in complete control and able to access this limitless power of your superconscious mind. I want you to be open and flow with this experience. You are always protected by the white light.

Now I would like you to ask your higher self to explore the origin of your fear of abandonment. Trust your higher self and your ability to allow any thoughts, feelings, or impressions to come into your subconscious mind concerning this goal. Do this now.

- PLAY NEW AGE MUSIC FOR 3 MINUTES

Now I would like you to let go of the situation, regardless of how simple or complicated it may seem. At this time I want you to visualize yourself in your daily life among all of those people with whom you have daily or occasional contact. Mentally create your new reality, free of any abandonment symptoms and with a new positive outlook on life.

- PLAY NEW AGE MUSIC FOR 4 MINUTES

You have done very well. Now I want you to further open up the channels of communication by removing any obstacles and allowing yourself to receive information and experiences that will directly apply to and help better your present lifetime. Allow yourself to receive more advanced and more specific information from your higher self and masters and guides to raise your frequency and improve your karmic subcycle. Do this now.

- PLAY NEW AGE MUSIC FOR 4 MINUTES

All right now. Sleep and rest. You did very well. Listen very carefully. I'm going to count forward now from 1 to 5. When I reach the count of 5 you will be back in the present; you will be able to remember everything you experienced and re-experienced. You'll feel very relaxed, refreshed, and you'll be able to do whatever you have planned for the rest of the day or evening. You'll feel positive about what you've just experienced and very motivated about your confidence and ability to play this tape again to experience your higher self. All right now. 1, very,

- very deep. 2, you're getting a little lighter. 3, you're
- much, much lighter. 4, very, very light. 5, awaken.
Wide awake and refreshed.

Agoraphobia

A forty-seven-year-old housewife suffered from agoraphobia for most of her adult life. She was afraid to leave her house and locked herself in her bedroom for most of the day. This pattern persisted for twelve years.

As a monk in the tenth century, he (she) had been forced into the clergy by his domineering father. He was persecuted by the Church for his opinions and eventually sent on one of the Crusades (Holy Wars). There he witnessed numerous killings and later went insane.

As a wealthy male landowner during the twelfth century in Southern France, he rebelled against an evil church official. This official tortured the landowner's daughter, causing her to become a "vegetable." The landowner cared for his incapacitated daughter for the rest of her life. When she finally died, he took action. He killed the church official and was executed for this murder.

Now listen very carefully. I want you to imagine a
bright white light, coming down from above and
- entering the top of your head, filling your entire
- body. See it, feel it, and it becomes reality. Now
- imagine an aura of pure white light emanating from
- your heart region, again surrounding your entire
- body, protecting you. See it, feel it, and it becomes a
- reality. Now only your higher self, masters and
- guides, and highly evolved loving entities who mean
- you well will be able to influence you during this or
- any other hypnotic session. You are totally protected
- by this aura of pure white light.

In a few moments, I am going to count from 1 to 20. As I do so you will feel yourself rising up to the super-conscious mind level where you will be able to receive information from your higher self and masters and guides. You will also be able to overview all of the past, present, and future lives. Number 1, rising up. 2, 3, 4, rising higher. 5, 6, 7, letting information flow. 8, 9, 10, you are halfway there. 11, 12, 13, feel yourself rising even higher. 14, 15, 16, almost there. 17, 18, 19, number 20, you are there. Take a moment and orient yourself to the superconscious mind level.

PLAY NEW AGE MUSIC FOR 1 MINUTE

You are now in a deep hypnotic trance, and from this superconscious mind level there is a complete understanding and resolution of your agoraphobia. Trust your higher self and your ability to allow any thoughts, feelings, or impressions to come into your subconscious mind concerning this goal. Do this now.

PLAY NEW AGE MUSIC FOR 3 MINUTES

Now I would like you to let go of the situation, regardless of how simple or complicated it may seem. Imagine each of your agoraphobic symptoms as a black and white photograph. Now perceive your actions when you are free of the symptoms as color photographs of yourself. Study the color photos. What led to this positive, symptom-free behavior? Place the pictures in a file labeled "the new me."

Now go through the black and white photos. Learn from this collection of dysfunctional behavior. The moment you learn from the experience, the unhappy memory serves no further usefulness and can be permanently discarded. The residue of discomfort can then be released from your mind.

Tie all these black and white photos together with a card on top that reads "the old me." Place this bundle in the garbage. Now put out the garbage.

PLAY NEW AGE MUSIC FOR 4 MINUTES

You have done very well. Now I want you to further open up the channels of communication by removing obstacles and allowing yourself to receive information and experiences that will directly apply to and improve your present lifetime. Allow yourself to receive more advanced and specific information from your higher self and masters and guides to raise your frequency and improve your karmic subcycle.

PLAY NEW AGE MUSIC FOR 4 MINUTES

All right now. Sleep and rest. You did very well. Listen very carefully. I'm going to count forward now from 1 to 5. When I reach the count of 5 you will be back in the present, and you will be able to remember everything you experienced and re-experienced. You'll feel very relaxed, refreshed, and you'll be able to do whatever you have planned for the rest of the day or evening. You'll feel positive about what you've just experienced and very motivated about your confidence and ability to play this tape again to experience your higher self. All right now. 1, very, very deep. 2, you're getting a little lighter. 3, you're much, much lighter. 4, very, very light. 5, awaken. Wide awake and refreshed.

Insomnia

A thirty-three-year-old art teacher came to me for help in overcoming her fear of having her throat cut. In bed at night she could not sleep unless she pulled the covers right up to her chin, covering her throat. She had nightmares and developed insomnia.

In a past life as Martinelli, a male monk working an Italian farm in the sixteenth century, my patient was a very happy man. One day while he was farming, soldiers attacked the monastery, killing all of the monks. A soldier grabbed him and cut his throat. After this regression, my patient's nightmares and insomnia disappeared.

In a different case, a twenty-seven-year-old woman, a benefits administrator, came to me, asking me to help her overcome the nightmares she was experiencing at night. She would wake up screaming *every night,* a pattern that had persisted for five years. After undergoing the following past life regressions, the nightmares and screaming disappeared completely.

First, in a frontier life, she was a male stable worker. He and his wife and child went for a ride one day, but their wagon ran into trouble on a high cliff. His wife and child fell to their deaths while my patient tried, unsuccessfully, to save them.

In a primitive life on a tropical island, she (as a male) was the people's leader. He opposed violence; when another tribe threatened his people, he counseled them to peaceably avoid conflict. His people rejected this advice, voting rather to stand and fight, whereupon they were soundly defeated, banished, and dispersed. Renegades from his former tribe forced him to lead a nocturnal attack against the aggressors. He (she) was caught and tortured to death by the enemy, culminating a night of ritualistic victory celebrations.

A thirty-eight-year-old housewife suffered from a severe case of insomnia. In 1880, she was a nun in Africa, aiding the village physician. Drums that the natives played kept her up at night. One day the doctor assisted in the stillborn delivery of the tribal chief's granddaughter. The nun and the doctor were tortured and killed.

Now listen very carefully. I want you to imagine a bright white light, coming down from above and entering the top of your head, filling your entire body. See it, feel it, and it becomes reality. Now imagine an aura of pure white light emanating from your heart region, again surrounding your entire body, protecting you. See it, feel it, and it becomes a reality. Now only your higher self, masters and guides, and highly evolved loving entities who mean you well will be able to influence you during this or any other hypnotic session. You are totally protected by this aura of pure white light.

In a few moments, I am going to count from 1 to 20. As I do so you will feel yourself rising up to the superconscious mind level, where you will be able to receive information from your higher self and masters and guides. You will also be able to overview all of your past, present, and future lives. Number 1, rising up. 2, 3, 4, rising higher. 5, 6, 7, letting information flow. 8, 9, 10, you are halfway there. 11, 12, 13, feel yourself rising even higher. 14, 15, 16, almost there. 17, 18, 19, number 20, you are there. Take a moment and orient yourself to the superconscious mind level.

PLAY NEW AGE MUSIC FOR 1 MINUTE

You are now in a deep hypnotic trance, and from this superconscious mind level there exists a complete understanding and resolution of the insomnia. You are in complete control and able to access this limitless power of your superconscious mind. I want you to be open and flow with this experience. You are always protected by the white light.

Now I would like you to ask your higher self to explore the origin of the insomnia. Trust your higher self and your own ability to allow any thoughts, feelings or impressions to come into your subconscious mind concerning this goal. Do this now.

PLAY NEW AGE MUSIC FOR 3 MINUTES

Now I would like you to let go of the situation, regardless of how simple or complicated it may seem. At this time I want you to visualize yourself free of this issue in your current life and consciousness.

Now imagine a scene that you find most pleasant...a scene that you would like to be in if you had a choice...as soon as your head touches the pillow at night you will re-create this positive scene and enter into hypnosis, then quickly into natural sleep.

If you should awaken in the middle of the night, you will not be disturbed...simply take a deep breath, hold it to the count of 6, let it out slowly and repeat the number 20 three times; you will enter into hypnosis again and then quickly drift into natural sleep.

You will fall asleep promptly and sleep soundly and restfully through the night. You will awaken in the morning refreshed, wide awake, and well rested.

PLAY NEW AGE MUSIC FOR 4 MINUTES

You have done very well. Now I want you to open up the channels of communication by removing any obstacles and allowing yourself to receive information and experiences that will directly apply to and help better your present lifetime. Allow yourself to receive more advanced and more specific information from your higher self and masters and guides to raise your frequency and improve your karmic sub-cycle. Do this now.

PLAY NEW AGE MUSIC FOR 4 MINUTES

All right now. Sleep and rest. You did very well. Listen very carefully. I'm going to count forward now from 1 to 5. When I reach the count of 5 you will be back in the present, and you will be able to remember everything you experienced and re-experienced. You will feel very relaxed, refreshed, and you'll be able to do whatever you have planned for the rest of the day or evening. You'll feel positive about what you've just experienced and very motivated about your confidence and ability to play this tape again to experience your higher self. All right now. 1, very, very deep. 2, you're getting a little lighter. 3, you're much, much lighter. 4, very, very light. 5, awaken. Wide awake and refreshed.

Stage Fright

A twenty-two-year-old female college senior came to me to help her overcome her stage fright. She was a theater major and apparently very talented. During rehearsals she could sing, act, and dance with absolutely no difficulties. However, it was during the actual performance that she would develop symptoms of severe stage fright.

In a past life in Russia, during the early 1900s, she was a member of an acting company. Her lover was also a member of the company. One day she discovered her lover was having a homosexual affair with the director. She was shocked and confronted him. He later committed suicide. The director discovered this, and she was arrested one night in mid-performance and shipped off to Siberia to live out a lonely and depressing existence. Her current drama coach at college was the Russian director in that earlier life.

A forty-five-year-old educator had a severe case of stage fright. She was regressed to a past life over 1,900 years earlier as a male preacher. He disagreed with the Church and spoke out against their policies and interpretation of the teachings of Christ. One day while preaching to the townspeople, he was attacked and killed.

Now listen very carefully. I want you to imagine a bright white light, coming down from above and entering the top of your head, filling your entire body. See it, feel it, and it becomes reality. Now imagine an aura of pure white light emanating from your heart region, again surrounding your entire body, protecting you. See it, feel it, and it becomes reality. Now only your higher self, masters and guides, and highly evolved loving entities who mean you well will be able to influence you during this or any other hypnotic session. You are totally protected by this aura of pure white light.

In a few moments, I am going to count from 1 to 20. As I do so you will feel yourself rising up to the superconscious mind level where you will be able to receive information from your higher self and masters and guides. You will also be able to overview all of your past, present, and future lives. Number 1, rising up. 2, 3, 4, rising higher. 5, 6, 7, letting information flow. 8, 9, 10, you are halfway there. 11, 12,

13, feel yourself rising even higher. 14, 15, 16, almost there. 17, 18, 19, number 20, you are there. Take a moment and orient yourself to the superconscious mind level

PLAY NEW AGE MUSIC FOR 1 MINUTE

You are now in a deep hypnotic trance, and from this superconscious mind level there exists a complete understanding and resolution of the stage fright. You are in complete control and able to access this limitless power of your superconscious mind. I want you to be open and flow with this experience. You are always protected by the white light.

At this time, ask your higher self to explore the origin of your stage fright. Trust your higher self and your own ability to allow any thoughts, feelings, or impressions to come into your subconscious mind concerning this goal. Do this now.

PLAY NEW AGE MUSIC FOR 3 MINUTES

Now I would like you to let go of the situation, regardless of how simple or complicated it may seem. At this time I want you to visualize yourself in your current life and consciousness, free of this issue. Perceive yourself getting up to give a talk.

The moment you get up to speak...all of your nervousness will disappear completely...and you will feel completely relaxed...completely at ease and completely confident. You will become so deeply interested in what you have to say...that the presence of the audience will no longer bother you in the slightest...and you will no longer feel uncertain...confused...or conspicuous in any way. Your mind will become so fully occupied with what you have to say that you will no longer feel nervous...self-conscious...or embarrassed...and you will remain throughout...perfectly calm...perfectly confident and self-assured.

Whenever you are called upon to give a speech or talk, remember you must thoroughly prepare for it. You must master the topic or become word-perfect if you are to recite something. Rehearse thoroughly before the actual presentation.

You will anticipate the performance with pleasurable expectation. During the performance, you will remain perfectly calm, poised, and self-confident. Your maximum ability and talents will surface.

Any nervousness or anxiety will be transferred to the little finger of your left hand, which will become stiff and rigid. As that temporary nervousness disappears, the finger will relax and return to normal.

Finally, perceive your speech being well received and you feeling confident about yourself and your presentation.

PLAY NEW AGE MUSIC FOR 4 MINUTES

You have done very well. Now I want you to further open up the channels of communication by removing any obstacles and allowing yourself to receive information and experiences that will directly apply to and help better your present lifetime. Allow

- yourself to receive more advanced and more specific
- information from your higher self and masters and
- guides to raise your frequency and improve your
- karmic subcycle. Do this now.
-
- PLAY NEW AGE MUSIC FOR 4 MINUTES
-
- All right now. Sleep and rest. You did very well. Lis-
- ten very carefully. I'm going to count forward now
- from 1 to 5. When I reach the count of 5 you will be
- back in the present, you will be able to remember
- everything you experienced and re-experienced.
- You'll feel very relaxed, refreshed, and you'll be able
- to do whatever you have planned for the rest of the
- day or evening. You'll feel positive about what
- you've just experienced and very motivated about
- your confidence and ability to play this tape again to
- experience your higher self. All right now. 1, very,
- very deep. 2, you're getting a little lighter. 3, you're
- much, much lighter. 4, very, very light. 5, awaken.
- Wide awake and refreshed.

Procrastination

A sixty-three-year-old female medical secretary wanted to overcome her tendency to procrastinate. In a past life as a Mexican
field worker with a wife and two children, with his friends he stole
goods and sold them on the black market to earn money to buy a
farm. His friends cheated him out of the money and told the
authorities that he was the only one who sold the goods. He was
imprisoned and worked on a chain gang. Later, he was transferred
to a fort where he saw his wife living with one of the soldiers. After
he was released from prison he joined the army and became a good
soldier. He was killed one day in an accidental explosion in the fort
while staying late to complete an assigned task.

Now listen very carefully. I want you to imagine a bright white light, coming down from above and entering the top of your head, filling your entire body. See it, feel it, and it becomes reality. Now imagine an aura of pure white light emanating from your heart region, again surrounding your entire body, protecting you. See it, feel it, and it becomes a reality. Now only your higher self, masters and guides, and highly evolved loving entities who mean you well will be able to influence you during this or any other hypnotic session. You are totally protected by this aura of pure white light.

In a few moments, I am going to count from 1 to 20. As I do so you will feel yourself rising up to the superconscious mind level where you will be able to receive information from your higher self and masters and guides. You will also be able to overview all of your past, present, and future lives. Number 1, rising up. 2, 3, 4, rising higher. 5, 6, 7, letting information flow. 8, 9, 10, you are halfway there. 11, 12, 13, feel yourself rising even higher. 14, 15, 16, almost there. 17, 18, 19, number 20, you are there. Take a moment and orient yourself to the superconscious mind level.

PLAY NEW AGE MUSIC FOR 1 MINUTE

At this time visualize yourself in your daily life motivated to do and complete all of the activities that must be done. In addition to those things you find pleasurable. Mentally create this new reality of yourself acting with confidence, empowerment, and an unlimited supply of energy as you accomplish each and every one of these goals, completely free of your former procrastination.

PLAY NEW AGE MUSIC FOR 4 MINUTES

You have done very well. Now I want you to further open up the channels of communication by removing any obstacles and allowing yourself to receive information and experiences that will directly apply to and help better your present lifetime. Allow yourself to receive more advanced and more specific information from your higher self and masters and guides to raise your frequency and improve your karmic subcycle. Do this now.

PLAY NEW AGE MUSIC FOR 4 MINUTES

All right now. Sleep and rest. You did very well. Listen very carefully. I'm going to count forward now from 1 to 5. When I reach the count of 5 you will be back in the present, you will be able to remember everything you experienced and re-experienced. You'll feel very relaxed, refreshed, and you'll be able to do whatever you have planned for the rest of the day or evening. You'll feel positive about what you've just experienced and very motivated about your confidence and ability to play this tape again to experience your higher self. All right now. 1, very, very deep. 2, you're getting a little lighter. 3, you're much, much lighter. 4, very, very light. 5, awaken. Wide awake and refreshed.

9

FUTURE LIFE PROGRESSIONS

The very idea of going forward in time has always fascinated humankind; at the same time it also frightens us. In the past only seers and psychics were supposed to have this "gift," and they were not always treated well by society. You literally risked your life by attempting to prognosticate the future.

Hypnotists and visionaries had long considered the possibility of going into the future, but scientific researchers considered the idea of such exploration merely a fantasy. H. G. Wells' *The Time Machine* stands out in many people's memories as an example of fictional time travel that just might be possible.

In 1977, while guiding one of my patients into hypnosis, I asked the woman to search for the true cause of her problem. I expected her to regress back into a previous lifetime, but instead she progressed into the twenty-third century. For me, this was the birth of progression hypnotherapy. I have done over 5,000 progressions since then, and have established this field as one based on reality, not mere fantasy.

In *Past Lives—Future Lives* (1988), I described a newscaster going into the future and documenting his progressions. In addition, many of my patients have reported back to me the eventual accuracy of their progressions.

I use the term "age progression" to describe going forward into the future of your current lifetime. Future life progression refers to moving ahead to an actual future life in a different physical body. The main difference between these two techniques is that future life progressions are far less stable than age progressions. When a subject moves forward in time in their current life, they are able to describe events that are happening around them in logical order. During a future life progression the scene may haphazardly shift from one environment to the other. This does not always occur, but it is almost unknown in the other techniques described.

THE CONCEPT OF FREQUENCIES

The concept of frequencies needs to be explained at this time. There is not just one future. The new physics clearly demonstrates the existence of parallel universes. Theoretically, there are an infinite number of parallel universes existing alongside ours. My experience in conducting progressions shows that there are five main paths, or frequencies. One of the many advantages of using progression hypnotherapy is to be able to lay out these five paths and choose your ideal path. This ideal frequency will then become your new reality. One of the case histories I describe in this chapter will illustrate this concept.

The new physics also teaches us that all past, present, and future events are happening at the same time. This is known as the space-time continuum, and it implies that the future influences the present as well as the past, and vice versa. This may sound confusing, but it does afford us the empowerment of changing our future by our current actions. The more you grow spiritually, the better your future frequencies are.

To illustrate the space-time continuum, imagine that you are driving your car on a highway. There is a helicopter 200 feet directly over your car. Both of your vehicles have a CB (citizen's band radio) and communicate with each other. Now add a car five miles behind your car (car A) and another car five miles ahead of you (car B) on this same highway. Each of these cars has a CB. You cannot see either of these cars because they are too far behind or ahead of you. The helicopter, because it is 200 feet above the highway, can easily see all these cars simultaneously.

This analogy now becomes even more interesting. The helicopter can communicate with you by way of the CB and inform you of an accident or other traffic problems where you came from (car A) or where you are going (car B). This same helicopter can also communicate with your past (car A) or future (car B) anytime it desires. When we enter into a hypnotic trance (alpha), we are actually undergoing an out-of-body experience and are placing ourselves in this helicopter above what I call "the highway of life."

Please note that in the following progression script you can go into the future of your current life (age progression) or a future incarnation (future life progression).

Progression Script

Now listen very carefully. I want you to imagine a bright white light, coming down from above and entering the top of your head, filling your entire body. See it, feel it, and it becomes reality. Now imagine an aura of pure white light emanating from your heart region, again surrounding your entire body, protecting you. See it, feel it, and it becomes a reality. Now only your higher self, masters and guides, and highly evolved loving entities who mean you well will be able to influence you during this or any other hypnotic session. You are totally protected by this aura of pure white light. Focus carefully on my voice as your subconscious mind's memory bank has memories of all past, present, and future lifetimes. This tape will help guide you into the future—the future of this life or the future of another lifetime. Shortly I will be counting forward from 1 to 20. Near the end of this count you are going to imagine yourself moving through a tunnel. Near the end of this count you will perceive the tunnel divide and veer off to the left and to the right. The right represents the past, the left represents the future. On the count of 20, you will perceive yourself in the future. Your subconscious and superconscious mind levels have all the knowledge and information that you desire. Carefully and comfortably feel yourself moving into the future with each count from 1 to 20. Listen carefully now. Number 1, feel yourself now moving forward to the future, into this very, very deep and dark tunnel. 2, 3, further and further and further into the future. It is a little bit disorienting, but you know you're moving into the future. 7, 8, 9, it's more stable now and you feel comfortable; you feel almost as if you're floating, as you're rising up and into the future. 10, 11, 12, the tunnel is now getting a little bit lighter and you can perceive a light at the end, another white light just like the white light that is surrounding you. 13, 14, 15, now you are almost there. Focus carefully. You can perceive a door in front of you to this left tunnel that you are in right now. The door will be opened in just a few moments and you will see yourself in the future. The words "sleep now and rest" will always detach you from any scene you are experiencing and allow you to await further instructions. 16, 17, it's very bright now and you are putting your hands on the door. 18, you open the door. 19, you step into this future, to this future scene. 20, carefully focus on your surroundings, look around you, see what you perceive. Can you perceive yourself? Can you perceive other people around you? Focus on the environment. What does it look like? Carefully focus on this. Use your complete objectivity. Block out any information from the past that might have interfered with the quality of the scene. Use only what your subconscious and superconscious mind level will observe. Now take a few moments, focus carefully on the scene, find out where you are and what you are doing, why you are there. Take a few moments; let the scene manifest itself.

PLAY NEW AGE MUSIC FOR 3 MINUTES

Now focus very carefully on what year this is. Think for a moment. Numbers will appear before your inner eyes. You will have knowledge of the year that you are in right now. Carefully focus on this year and these numbers. They will appear before you. Use this as an example of other information that you are going to obtain. I want you to perceive this scene completely, carrying it through to completion. I want you to perceive exactly where you are, who you are, the name, the date, the place. I want you to carry these scenes to completion, follow them through carefully for the next few moments. The scene will become clear and you will perceive the sequence of what exactly is happening to you.

PLAY NEW AGE MUSIC FOR 3 MINUTES

You've done very well. Now you are going to move to another event. I want you to focus on a difference in the same future time. Perceive what is going on and why this is important to you. Perceive the year, the environment, and the presence of others. Let the information flow.

PLAY NEW AGE MUSIC FOR 3 MINUTES

As you perceive the details of the next scene, focus on your purpose in this future time, and how it is affecting your karmic subcycle. Focus in on what you are learning, and what you are unable to learn. Perceive any sequence of events that led up to this situation. Let the information flow surrounding this all-important future event now.

PLAY NEW AGE MUSIC FOR 3 MINUTES

You have done very well. Now I want you to rise to the superconscious mind level to evaluate this future experience and apply this knowledge to your current life and situations. 1, rising up. 2, rising higher. 3, halfway there. 4, almost there. 5, you are there. Let your masters and guides assist you in making the most out of this experience. Do this now.

> All right now. Sleep and rest. You did very well. Listen very carefully. I'm going to count forward now from 1 to 5. When I reach the count of 5 you will be back in the present, and you will be able to remember everything you experienced and re-experienced. You'll feel very relaxed, refreshed, and you'll be able to do whatever you have planned for the rest of the day or evening. You'll feel positive about what you've just experienced and very motivated about your confidence and ability to play this tape again to experience additional future events. All right now. 1, very, very deep. 2, you're getting a little lighter. 3, you're much, much lighter. 4, very, very light. 5, awaken.

FUTURE LIFE PROGRESSION CASES

In this section we will deal with lifetimes that occur in centuries yet to come.

A Contaminated Future Life

Pete, a clinical psychologist, called me in August of 1984 for help with his hand-washing compulsion. He knew all about compulsions, but could not help himself. Pete had spent years in therapy with no results. He would constantly wash his hands, day and night. He also changed his clothes two to three times a day to "remove the dirt." There was absolutely no logic to his fear of contamination or his feeling that if he didn't go through his daily rituals he wouldn't be able to function.

Another unusual aspect of Pete's psychological profile was the number 8. This number haunted him. He was born in August (the eighth month). Every time he obtained a new telephone number or a new address, the number 8 was always there. His grandmother had died in August, as had many other members of his family. In addition, the name Teresa seemed to haunt him throughout his current life.

In Pete's case, the most significant cause of his problem turned out to be a future lifetime.

Dr. G.: What is your name?

Pete: Ben. Ben Kingsley.

Dr. G.: Where do you find yourself?

Pete: I'm in school, and I like what I'm studying.

Dr. G.: What is it that you are studying?

Pete: It's a science course, and I like the work.

Dr. G.: Where do you live, Ben?

Pete: Tulsa. Tulsa, Oklahoma.

Dr. G.: What year is this?

Pete: 2074.

Dr. G.: What do you want to do with your life?

Pete: I want to go to college and do something in a scientific field. I don't know exactly which field yet.

Dr. G.: How do you like school?

Pete: I love it.

Dr. G.: What is your major?

Pete: Now I'm concentrating in nuclear physics.

Dr. G.: With what goal?

Pete: When I graduate I want to work as a technician in a nuclear power plant.

Dr. G.: With all your skills, why not become a nuclear physicist?

Pete: I couldn't do that.

Dr. G.: Why not?

Pete: Because I'm not cut out for that kind of responsibility.

Dr. G.: Don't you think you could handle the training?

Pete: I'm sure I could. But, you see, I get a little nervous sometimes when things don't go well.

Dr. G.: What do you mean by a little nervous?

Pete: Well, every once in a while, when I get nervous and frustrated, I develop a panicky feeling.

Dr. G.: What do you do?

Pete: I lose my temper sometimes, and don't think too clearly for a few minutes.

Dr. G.: This sounds like a real problem. Have you told your father about this?

Pete: Yes, he knows about it.

Dr. G.: Has he done anything about it?

Pete: I am seeing one of his colleagues, a Dr. Margolis.

Dr. G.: What does Dr. Margolis tell you about your condition?

Pete: He tells me it's not very serious, but that I should keep my stress levels down and to avoid repeated confrontations.

Dr. G.: Doesn't that preclude a career as a nuclear plant technician?

Pete: It would if it was found out, but that won't be a problem.

Dr. G.: How so?

Pete: Dr. Margolis is a very good friend of my father. He owes Dad a big favor. Also, he is well aware of my academic record.

Dr. G.: By that you mean he will keep your therapy off the record.

Pete: That's correct.

Ben was a very happy man. He graduated from college and married Gail. His family was proud of him, and he was well on his way to achieving his lifelong goals. I next progressed him to his working environment.

Dr. G.: Tell me about your work.

Pete: I absolutely love it. I work as a technician in the nuclear plant outside of Tulsa.

As I progressed Ben forward in time, he reported a deep love for his life. Although his family was important to him, his dedication was to his job. In fact, I perceived a little too much dedication. Ben had an obsessive-compulsive personality, which is not uncommon among scientifically trained people. What concerned me were the excessive workaholic traits he was exhibiting, coupled with a high-strung nature that was potentially explosive and dangerous.

I progressed him to a significant event in dealing with his emotions and his temper.

Dr. G.: Where are you now, Ben?

Pete: I'm home and arguing with Gail.

Dr. G.: What is this all about?

Pete: She got into a car accident. It was so stupid. She just ran out of the house after we had words and didn't think clearly about other vehicles.

Dr. G.: Was she hurt?

Pete: No, thank goodness.

Dr. G.: Did you have a temper episode?

Pete: Yes, and Gail was shocked. She didn't really think it
was a serious matter. She just wrote it off to the accident
itself.

Dr. G.: Have you now thought of seeing Dr. Margolis?

Pete: No, and I don't want to be told about me going back
into therapy. Is that understood?

Ben was getting very emotional about his psychological state.
He even threatened me. After years of calm, the storm began to
rise on the horizon. I could understand his concern about his
career, but felt he was acting irresponsibly in refusing to go back to
Dr. Margolis. His therapy could still be kept confidential.

Ben's life quieted down over the next year or so. He felt better
and naturally assumed there would be no further problems. I
didn't assume that at all.

Dr. G.: What is your career like now?

Pete: I have been promoted to chief technician at the
research facility.

Dr. G.: Is this work classified?

Pete: No. We just research safe and more effective uses of
nuclear power.

Dr. G.: What does the facility look like?

Pete: We have a rather large building, subdivided into various corridors. Each corridor represents a different division
and all divisions are color-coded.

Dr. G.: Do these divisions have names?

Pete: Yes, of course. There is Norad-Alpha and Norad-Beta,
Gama-Alpha and Gama-Beta, and my unit is Teres-Alpha.

Dr. G.: Is there a Teres-Beta?

Pete: Yes. Didn't I mention that? I apologize for the oversight.

Dr. G.: Do you occasionally make small oversights at work?

Pete: Now, don't you start that again (getting angry)! I am competent to do my work, and I don't need to see Dr. Margolis.

Dr. G.: I didn't say anything about Dr. Margolis.

Pete: I know, but you were going to, weren't you?

Dr. G.: Ben, have you had any difficulties at all at work?

Pete: Sometimes I miss on a calculation and my men correct me.

Dr. G.: Does that get you angry?

Pete: Not enough that it shows. But yes, I do get down on myself.

Dr. G.: Are you a perfectionist?

Pete: I don't think so. I just want everything to be done correctly.

Dr. G.: What is the difference?

Pete: I guess none. I will admit to being a perfectionist. Does that make me mentally unfit?

Dr. G.: It could, if it makes you angry enough to let your emotions rule your behavior unchecked.

Pete: Well, that doesn't happen, so I guess I'm OK.

Ben went on to tell me more about his position. He was in charge of the Teres-Alpha division, which dealt with researching ways to contain nuclear power and eliminate nuclear waste products more effectively. He was indeed a good supervisor—young, aggressive, knowledgeable, and totally dedicated. If you could ignore his emotional problems, he was perfect for the job. I could not ignore his psychological profile, and my concern was growing by the minute.

As I progressed him forward, he described his many activities at the facility. He sat in on board meetings, participated in planning major projects, correlated the data from his division, and handled public relations, among other things. In short, Ben had a lot of responsibilities. Considering his emotional state, I felt he was biting off more than he could chew. I asked him to go forward to the most significant event in that life.

Dr. G.: What year is this, Ben?

Pete: 2088.

Dr. G.: What's going on in your life at this time?

Pete: I'm really excited about my project.

Dr. G.: What is it, exactly?

Pete: I'm working on a way to compartmentalize and quantify the flow of nuclear material from one reactor site to another.

Dr. G.: That sounds complicated and dangerous.

Pete: It is. But it's also exciting.

Dr. G.: Are all of your men working on this project?

Pete: No, just me and Ralph. I do most of the calculations.

Dr. G.: Are you putting in a lot of overtime on this?

Pete: Yes.

Dr. G.: Have there been any problems?

Pete: Just the usual frustrations—nothing major.

Dr. G.: Does Ralph work overtime with you?

Pete: No, he goes home on time. I stay late by myself.

Dr. G.: So you do work better when you're alone?

Pete: You know, I never thought about it, but I do. I really do like it better at night when only a skeleton crew is around.

Dr. G.: You mean there aren't people working there at night.

Pete: No, not really. We have the usual security people on board in the evening, but very few researchers or technicians are around at night.

I now progressed Ben forward to an actual event that would be meaningful to him. He reported being at the facility late one evening in 2088. He was alone, and there were some problems.

Dr. G.: What is it, Ben?

Pete: Something is very wrong here.

Dr. G.: Exactly what is it that's wrong?

Pete: The level of nuclear wastes has risen, and the diffraction chamber I developed isn't working.

Dr. G.: What do you mean, isn't working?

Pete: Apparently, my calculations were off and there's an overflow of the backup of these waste products.

Dr. G.: Can you handle this emergency?

Pete: I'm sure I can. Wait…it isn't working! What am I going to do?

Dr. G.: Move forward, calmly, to your actions.

Pete: The dials are going crazy. The danger signal is about to be reached.

Dr. G.: Can you call for help?

Pete: I can handle this. I can do this myself. After all, I am the chief technician.

Dr. G.: Go on.

Pete: It's no use. The system is backing up.

Dr. G.: What do you do?

Pete: The signal has sounded. The security men will be here shortly. I can't let them see what I've done.

Dr. G.: What will you do?

Pete: I will isolate myself from them.

Dr. G.: Is there anybody with you now?

There was silence for a very long two minutes. When Ben finally responded, he described a bizarre set of circumstances. There was a security guard making his rounds in the Teres-Alpha unit. Ben knocked him unconscious with a hard metal object. He then went completely out of control. The frustration of his personal failure had gotten to him. Ben couldn't handle the situation. It was his fault that this meltdown and contamination were occurring. He alone had handled the calculations that resulted in misprogramming the computer. When he calmed down, I continued the questioning.

Dr. G.: What is happening now, Ben?

Pete: I'm totally isolated. I've sealed off this unit, and it will take hours for them to get in here.

Dr. G.: What will that solve?

Pete: Nothing, but I must be alone.

Dr. G.: What have you done to correct the situation?

Pete: I turned all of the power and diffraction switches on high.

Dr. G.: Won't that add to the overload?

Pete: It sure will. This baby will blow, and I'm going with it.

Dr. G.: Don't you want this to end a different way?

Pete: No. Nobody is going to fire me. Nobody is going to tell me I was wrong.

Dr. G.: What about the guard and the others?

Pete: I don't care. I don't care.

Ben had a nervous breakdown. Pete, sitting in my recliner, was in no danger. It was Ben who couldn't listen to reason. As a result of his actions, there was a complete meltdown of the research facility. The skeleton crew and Ben were killed. The nuclear contamination from Ben's miscalculations affected the entire Tulsa area. The water supply was contaminated. So were the food supplies, and so was everything else. I spoke to Ben from the superconscious mind level.

Dr. G.: Ben, what did you learn from this?

Pete: I learned how to contaminate a major city by my stupidity. I learned nothing but how to hurt innocent people.

Ben didn't quite understand another connection from this future life. He died in August of the year 2088. The eighth month and the year 2088 were significant associations to the number 8. In addition, Ben worked in the Teres-Alpha unit. This spells out as Teresa, a name that haunted Pete most of his life.

Pete was brought out of his trance, feeling drained and unsure of what this all meant. I told him that this future life was the real cause of his present contamination compulsion and explained the origin of his difficulties with the number 8 and the name Teresa.

Pete was still confused. How could this future life help him now? He didn't want to experience that terrible life a hundred years from now. I agreed with him. Although I did effect some cleansing from the superconscious mind level, that wouldn't solve his problem. The answer lay in the application of the principles of quantum physics.

That future was just one of at least five major probabilities. Pete had perceived a negative frequency , or probability, though he had at least four others from which to choose. The solution to his problem was really quite simple: All I had to do was to have him preview the other four choices and then, after he selected the ideal frequency, program that frequency to be his reality. By doing this I would help Pete to switch frequencies so his future would be quite different than it was sure to be if we did nothing.

You may ask how I can do this. How can I change the future? What you must consider is that every time you make a choice you are, in effect, changing the future. In Pete's case, progressing him to the other parallel existences he would have at the end of the twenty-first century would accomplish that very goal.

Pete progressed nicely to four other lifetimes in that same time frame. After each life was reviewed, he carefully selected the one he felt was ideal, and I then progressed him to that frequency. The various environmental factors can be quite similar in these parallel frequencies, as was the case here. However, there will always be major differences, and each action by Pete in a certain frequency will have a specific effect on the total outcome of his life.

There is no predestination. The soul always has free will. What is somewhat predestined is the basic framework of the frequency. The specifics can be changed by varying the choices along the way, but the basic framework can't be altered. You cannot just choose the best aspects of all five frequencies. You can only choose one frequency and accept the good with the bad. That is one reason I always have the patient make the choice.

I won't bore you with the details of Pete's other frequencies — I'll just tell you the one he chose. Remember, the basic environmental details were similar; his name, family members, and parents' occupation were identical. It was Ben himself in this ideal frequency who showed some noticeable difference.

Dr. G.: Where are you now, Ben?

Pete: I'm a senior in college.

Dr. G.: What is your major?

Pete: Nuclear physics.

Dr. G.: With what goal?

Pete: I want to go to graduate school and become a nuclear physicist.

Dr. G.: Do you ever get upset and lose control of your temper?

Pete: No. What a silly thing that is to ask.

In this frequency, Ben didn't settle for being just a technician. He went for the brass ring and became a nuclear physicist. In addition, he didn't exhibit any of the signs of emotional instability that he had shown in the previous frequency. Thus, there were no visits to Dr. Margolis and no temper episodes.

This frequency was indeed ideal and different. By August of 2088 things were very different. Ben had no emotional problems. All of the previous frequency's problems seem to have been avoided.

I next progressed Ben to the end of 2088.

Dr. G.: Tell me about your work.

Pete: I have been working on a technique to help divert nuclear waste safely and to more effectively contain nuclear power.

Dr. G.: How is it going?

Pete: Quite well. Thanks to an excellent staff and my good friend, Ralph, we have successfully tested the techniques.

Dr. G.: So, is it a success?

Pete: A great success.

Dr. G.: What is the name of your unit?

Pete: Why, it's called Teres-Alpha.

So the pattern was complete.

Pete passed the magical year of 2088 without causing the disaster in which he had participated in the previous frequency. He, as Ben, still worked in Teres-Alpha, but that name didn't act as a jinx. In fact, you might say it was a good-luck charm.

Pete made rapid progress after this session. He no longer feared the number 8 or the name Teresa. He understood what they really meant and why the contamination compulsion had been so deeply ingrained within his psyche. Pete today is totally recovered. He accomplished this himself with a little assistance from progression therapy. I like this case because it illustrates the principle that the future is now. We can change the future, but we must perceive it first.

Emily came to me in the summer of 1981. Her chief complaint was ulcerative colitis. This gastrointestinal disorder is described as a chronic, non-specific, inflammatory and ulcerative disease of the colon characterized most often by bloody diarrhea. This disease most frequently begins between the ages of fifteen and forty. The cause is unknown. The syndrome is most uncomfortable, as it consists of an increased need to defecate, mild lower abdominal cramps, and the appearance of blood and mucus in the stool. It is not uncommon for a patient to have ten to twenty bowel movements per day, often accompanied by severe cramps. A great concern is the possibility of colon cancer. Since we know stress brings on colitis attacks, tracing the source of the stress and reprogramming it would literally solve Emily's problem.

The true origin of Emily's stress rested in the thirty-sixth century. She lived on Phonican, a planet in the Andromeda System. Her name was Sequestra and her people were enslaved by a fanatical group called the Aracatha. Sequestra was valuable to them because she was "keeper of the knowledge," and her mind stored priceless scientific data.

The Aracatha were pure energy, so they used Sequestra's people to experiment with the concept of being in a body for a time. Sequestra was assigned to head a research project to create genetically perfect bodies for the Aracatha to use at their pleasure. In reality, she led an underground resistance movement whose goal was to forever rid her people of the tyrannical Aracatha oppressors.

When I asked Sequestra what her plan was, she told me, "The karmic cycle is our only salvation. There are sixteen members of the Aracatha, and their goal is to occupy a human body at will. When I assist in the perfection of the technique, I know each member of the Aracatha will immediately play with their new toy. They will all enter a body and play."

The brilliance of her plan centered on a resonance frequency device she developed, which trapped the Aracatha one by one within the bodies they entered. Her plan was carried and it worked like clockwork.

While the Aracatha occupied their respective bodies, they had already begun to illustrate the genius of Sequestra's plan. They participated in unusual sexual practices, murdered some of Sequestra's people for sport, and generally incurred some heavy karmic debts. They were exiled to a small asteroid to live out the rest of their lives. Emily truly benefitted from the progression aspect of my therapy. She is now free of colitis and has a new lease on life.

JERRY SPRINGER'S FUTURE LIFE

Television personality Jerry Springer's attitude toward the possibility of viewing his next lifetime can best be summed up by the term "healthy skeptic." However, at the outset of progression therapy, he did not think he would be capable of viewing the future, an opinion he soon recanted.

In the latter part of the next century, Jerry will be a rancher/farmer named Bobby, working in Montana. He is married and has four children. Bobby is involved with a government project designed to raise crops on our moon. He will be killed at the age of sixty when his craft crashes during a return trip to Earth.

Two interesting facts surfaced from this future life progression. First, Jerry's future-life wife is a girl he knew in high school named Robin. Second, he stated on his show that to this day he is afraid to dive into a pool. This phobia has led to much embarrassment during past vacations.

A PARALLEL LIFE

Not only do we have past and future lives, but our soul (which is energy in the form of electromagnetic radiation) is capable of occupying more than one physical body in our current life. When we perceive these parallel universes in progression therapy, the purpose is to choose the ideal one for our spiritual growth. These universes are in the future of our current life, or in future lifetimes in centuries to come. In rare instances, an individual can meet another body in their current life whose energy (soul) is identical with theirs. Both of these souls originated from a common ancestor. We shall call this common ancestor the "Oversoul."

Such was the case several years ago with a salesman patient of mine. He learned of his parallel self though a superconscious mind tap. This patient informed me that his "alter ego" was a woman living in Cleveland, Ohio.

This male patient had never been to Cleveland but did have occasion to go to Cincinnati for some of his sales calls. Since he had retrieved the complete name and address of his "parallel self," it was not difficult to look her up during his next trip to the Midwest.

By using his persuasive personality, my patient arranged to meet with this woman. He described a most unusual evening "date" with *himself*. They chatted and eventually parted company. Their incredible similarities, accompanied by very "strange feelings," were too much for them to deal with emotionally.

We all have parallel selves, but most of us will never meet them. The following figures explain how this occurs.

In Figure 5 (below), we see that an oversoul splits into three subsouls. Each subsoul further divides itself into three additional subsouls, and so on. If our salesman and the Cleveland woman's soul originated from subsoul 1 (as in Figure 5A), you can note the common background for the respective energy component (soul).

This concept (known as the Oversoul Concept) helps explain the world's population and lack of virgin (new) souls today. One oversoul dividing into just three subsouls and each subsoul also occupying three physical bodies would result in the same original oversoul occupying over 1.5 million bodies in just thirteen generations (480 years).

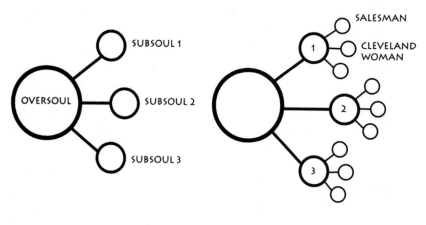

Figure 5   **Figure 5A**

The Oversoul Concept

10

ANGEL ENCOUNTERS

Angels have an erratic history in our society. These spiritual beings guard the east gates of Eden with flashing swords in Genesis (Old Testament). They do battle with a dragon in Revelation (New Testament). The Bible more often portrays angels as combative entities.

New Agers have a completely different concept of angels. According to Angelologists, angels are wise and loving beings who are non-threatening; angels guide us, and their only message is love.

Three of the major religions, Christianity, Islam, and Judaism, incorporate angels as part of their theology. Angels also appear in Hinduism, Buddhism, and Zoroastrianism. You will find angel references in over half of the Bible. An angel saved Daniel from the lion's den, told Abraham to spare his own son from sacrifice, and it was an angel who rolled the stone away from Christ's tomb.

During medieval times, angels were situated as a buffer between humankind and God. Angels were said to rotate the planets, make plants grow, and move the stars. The writings of fifth-century theologian Dionysus inspired a classification system for an angel hierarchy. In descending order of rank, they are:

- Seraphim, Cherubim, and Thrones. The thrones are responsible for bringing justice.

- Dominion, Virtues (they work miracles), and Powers (these angels protect humankind from evil).

- Principalities (they concern themselves with the welfare of nations), Archangels, and Angels. These last two serve as guides and messengers to humans.

Angels are neither gods nor ghosts. These beings were created separately from humans and were given free will. This explains Satan as a fallen angel. Angels have consciousness and purpose. They are organized to grow in consciousness and achieve goals. Some describe these beings as "extra-cosmic intelligence."

The celestial beings appear in the life form of a body only in order to carry out a task. They may appear in our dreams.

Angels have no gender or corporeal (physical) body; they are pure spirit and were never a part of humankind. We don't become an angel when we cross into spirit, according to theologians.

Angels exist because of our faith in them. In *A Book of Angels* (Ballantine, 1990), author Sophy Burnham states that angels disguise themselves—as a dream, a comforting presence, a pulse of energy, a person—to ensure that the message is received, even if the messenger is explained away. "It is not that skeptics do not experience the mysterious and divine," she explains, "but rather that the mysteries are presented to them in such a flat and factual, everyday, reasonable way so as not to disturb." The rule, she says, is that people receive only as much information as they can bear, in the form they can stand to hear it.

Angels do not interfere with our free will; they merely advise and support us. We must have pure motives for an angel contact to occur. This communication must be part of God's plan and we must be prepared for an encounter.

These beings of pure spirit reassure us that God is real and filled with miraculous powers. Any angelic message always leaves us with confidence and helps us better ourselves in some way. These messages are designed to give us the right and freedom to choose our actions.

To invite an encounter with an angel through hypnosis is not much different from a superconscious mind tap. You will note some minor differences in the following script:

Angel Encounters Script

Now listen very carefully. I want you to imagine a bright white light coming down from above and entering the top of your head, filling your entire body. See it, feel it, and it becomes reality. Now imagine an aura of pure white light emanating from your heart region, again surrounding your entire body, protecting you. See it, feel it, and it becomes reality. Now only your angels and highly evolved loving entities who mean you well will be able to influence you during this or any other hypnotic session. You are totally protected by this aura of pure white light.

In a few moments, I am going to count from 1 to 20. As I do so, you will feel yourself rising up to the superconscious mind level, where you will be able to receive information from your angel protectors. Number 1 rising up. 2, 3, 4, rising higher. 5, 6, 7, letting information flow. 8, 9, 10, you are halfway there. 11, 12, 13, feel yourself rising even higher. 14, 15, 16, almost there. 17, 18, 19, number 20 and you are there. Take a moment and orient yourself to the superconscious mind level.

PLAY NEW AGE MUSIC FOR 1 MINUTE

You may contact any of your angels from this level. You may explore your relationship with any person. Remember, your superconscious mind level is all knowledgeable and has access to your akashic records. Let your higher self send out the appropriate energy to attract one of your angels.

Now slowly and carefully state your desire for information or an experience and let this superconscious mind level work for you.

PLAY NEW AGE MUSIC FOR 8 MINUTES

You have done very well. Now I want you to further open up the channels of communication by removing any obstacles and allowing yourself to receive information and experiences that will directly apply to and help better your present lifetime. Allow yourself to receive more advanced and more specific information from your higher self and angels to raise your frequency and improve your karmic subcycle. Do this now.

PLAY NEW AGE MUSIC FOR 8 MINUTES

All right now. Sleep and rest. You did very well. Listen very carefully. I'm going to count forward now from 1 to 5. When I reach the count of 5, you will be

- back in the present; you will be able to remember
- everything you experienced and re-experienced.
- You'll feel very relaxed, refreshed, and you'll be able
- to do whatever you have planned for the rest of the
- day or evening. You'll feel very positive about what
- you've just experienced and very motivated about
- your confidence and ability to play this tape again to
- experience your angels. All right now. 1, very, very
- deep. 2, you're getting a little bit lighter. 3, you're
- getting much, much lighter. 4, very light. 5, awaken.
  Wide awake and refreshed.

OUT-OF-BODY EXPERIENCE

Since an angel encounter often occurs during an out-of-body experience, I present the following script for you to practice:

Now listen very carefully. I want you to imagine a bright white light coming down from above and
- entering the top of your head, filling your entire
- body. See it, feel it, and it becomes reality. Now
  imagine an aura of pure white light emanating from
- your heart region, again surrounding your entire
  body, protecting you. See it, feel it, and it becomes
  reality. Now only your masters and guides and high-
- ly evolved loving entities who mean you well will be
- able to influence you during this or any other hyp-
- notic session. You are totally protected by this aura
- of pure white light.

- Now as you focus in on how comfortable and relaxed
- you are, free of distractions, free from physical and

emotional obstacles that prevent you from safely leaving and returning to the physical body, you will perceive and remember all that you encounter during this experience. You will recall in detail when you are physically awake only these matters which will be beneficial to your physical and mental being and experience. Now begin to sense the vibrations around you, and in your own mind begin to shape and pull them into a ring around your head. Do this for a few moments now.

PLAY NEW AGE MUSIC FOR 2 MINUTES

Now as you begin to attract these vibrations into your inner awareness, they begin to sweep throughout your body, making it rigid and immobile. You are always in complete control of this experience. Do this now as you perceive yourself rigid and immobile, with these vibrations moving along and throughout your entire body.

PLAY NEW AGE MUSIC FOR 3 MINUTES

You have done very well. Pulse these vibrations. Perceive yourself feeling the pulse of these vibrations throughout your entire awareness. In your own mind's eye, reach out with one arm and grasp some object that you know is out of normal reach. Feel the object and let your astral hand pass through it. Your mind is using your astral arm, not your physical arm, to feel the object. As you do this, you are becoming lighter and your astral body is beginning to rise up from your physical body. Do this now.

- **PLAY NEW AGE MUSIC FOR 3 MINUTES**

  You've done very well. Now, using other parts of your astral body (your head, feet, chest, and back), repeat this exercise and continue to feel lighter and lighter as your astral body begins to rise up from your physical body. Do this now.

- **PLAY NEW AGE MUSIC FOR 3 MINUTES**

  Now think of yourself as becoming lighter and lighter throughout your body. Perceive yourself as your entire astral body lifts up and floats away from your physical body. Concentrate on blackness and remove all fears during this process. Imagine a helium-filled balloon rising and pulling with it your astral body, up and away from your physical body. Do this now.

- **PLAY NEW AGE MUSIC FOR 3 MINUTES**

  Now orient yourself to this new experience. You are out of your body, relaxed, safe, and totally protected by the white light. Concentrate on a place, not far away, that you would like to visit with your astral body. Now go to this place. Do this now. Perceive this new environment.

- **PLAY NEW AGE MUSIC FOR 3 MINUTES**

  You've done very well. Now I want you to travel to a destination much farther away. It can be a location across the country or anywhere around the world. Think of this destination and you will be there in just a few moments. Do this now.

- PLAY NEW AGE MUSIC FOR 3 MINUTES
- All right now. Sleep and rest. You did very well. Lis-
- ten very carefully. I'm going to count forward now
- from 1 to 5. When I reach the count of 5, you will be
- back in your body, you will be able to remember
- everything you experienced and re-experienced.
- You'll feel very relaxed, refreshed, and you'll be able
- to do whatever you have planned for the rest of the
- day or evening. You'll feel very positive about what
- you've just experienced and very motivated about
- your confidence and ability to play this tape again to
- experience leaving your physical body safely. All
- right now. 1, very, very deep. 2, you're getting a lit-
- tle bit lighter. 3, you're getting much, much lighter.
- 4, very, very light. 5, awaken. Wide awake and
- refreshed.

AN ANGEL IN UNIFORM

Marissa was eighteen years old when she had an angelic interven-
tion that saved her from a most traumatic experience. She was a
virgin and a devout Christian. Marissa's best friend, Carla, was
quite the opposite, and repeatedly tempted Marissa into "broad-
ening her horizons" with sex and drugs. Carla slept around,
smoked pot, and occasionally used cocaine. Marissa had never
tried drugs and wouldn't even drink alcohol. The only reason
Marissa associated with Carla was because Marissa had no other
friends. One day Carla invited Marissa to a party at her home in
Los Angeles. Carla's parents were in Palm Springs for the weekend,
so they had the place to themselves.

When Marissa arrived, she was shocked. In addition to the
presence of over 150 people at the party (she had been told only

a dozen or so were invited), there were drugs all over the place. People were smoking pot, popping pills, and even syringes were in use.

Todd and James were two of Carla's best friends. They quickly led Marissa to the den to show her something Carla had made for her. As Carla painted for a hobby, this was not a suspicious request.

While in the den, Todd and James tore Marissa's blouse off and announced they were going to rape her. Marissa froze and prayed for a moment. A loud knock at the front door changed everything. A man announced, "This is the police—open this door!" Marissa noted his name, badge number, and patrol car number and left. She did not file any charges against Todd or James.

A few days later Marissa called the precinct to express her gratitude to the officer. She was amazed to learn that the police had no record of an officer with his name. The patrol car number and badge number were not on their records, either. No official call was made or reported to Carla's house that night.

When Marissa told me of this incident four years later in my office, she asked me who this man could possibly be. I informed her that it was probably her "guardian angel." Today, Marissa is married and the proud mother of a baby boy. Yes, she did remain a virgin until her wedding night as she purposed. She also married a man of similar qualities and they are both very happy.

The case illustrates a different type of healing. This form is preventive. Marissa's angel (or manifestation of her higher self or guide) saved her from a physically, emotionally, and spiritually traumatic encounter. I do not doubt for one moment that she would have been severely compromised by the rape and other abuse Todd and James would have perpetrated upon her.

This experience has resulted in a further strengthening of Marissa's belief in God and in the power of faith.

THE HOLLYWOOD ANGEL

Since my practice is located in Woodland Hills, California (a suburb of Los Angeles), a certain percentage of my local patients remind me where I live by their experiences. Sam was a salesman living in Hollywood, California. His neighborhood was a rough one where crime was rampant and drug deals were consummated on local street corners and in alleys.

It was Sam's habit to walk to a local convenience store to get cigarettes in the evening. Although he had lived in this dangerous neighborhood for several years, Sam had never had any problems with criminals. One fateful evening in September of 1994, he was approached by three would-be muggers on the way to his favorite convenience store. One of his potential assailants pulled out a knife and demanded Sam's wallet. The other laughed and told Sam they were going to "hurt him bad."

The next thing he remembered was the appearance of a tall, thin man in his early thirties who stood between Sam and the muggers. The muggers looked at this stranger and stood motionless. Sam ran to freedom, but upon looking back toward the tall stranger, he was shocked. The stranger just disappeared into thin air while the muggers stood almost frozen.

To this day, Sam still can't explain what happened. This "angel" clearly saved Sam's life. I call that the ultimate form of healing.

■ ■ ■

11

FINDING A QUALIFIED HYPNOTHERAPIST

I have always been a great advocate of formal scientific training. Perhaps my degrees in biochemistry, dentistry, and counseling psychology favorably predispose me in this direction; but all prejudice aside, education does serve a purpose. In an ideal world, your prospective hypnotherapist would be trained in psychology and/or medicine, but many of the techniques practiced today find no formal counterparts in the traditional curricula.

In the absence of this training, or even in its presence, certain criteria for evaluating a clinician should be employed. First, they should never, under any circumstances, require recreational drugs, especially hallucinogenic agents, as part of their therapy. The purpose of hypnotherapy is to bring one's energy into balance and raise its quality. No drug can do that for you.

If such a therapist refuses to disclose the names of former patients, do not be alarmed. Confidentiality is part and parcel of professional therapy, and in fact, enjoys statutory protection in all fifty states. However, your prospective clinician should not exhibit "plaqueaphobia." By this term, I mean an explicit aversion to having anyone closely inspect the degree(s) mounted on the office wall. If the clinician advertises the trappings of a formal education, what could be wrong with examining the diplomas attesting to that education? Natural curiosity impels us to study a professional's background accreditation. The problem is that if these are phony, spurious degrees purchased from a diploma mill, the hypnotist will not want you to discover this particular skeleton in his or her closet.

As far as bona fide degrees are concerned, a psychiatrist holds an M.D. degree; a psychologist possesses a Ph.D. or Psy. D. or Ed.D. (Doctorate of Education); counselors usually have an M.F.C.C., M.C. or M.A. degree; social workers earn an M.S.W. or D.S.W.; pastoral counselors can have any combination of these degrees or possess a D.D. (Doctor of Divinity); dentists hold a D.D.S. or D.M.D. degree. Make sure the university the practitioner claims as his or her alma mater is accredited. Your local library can help you find this out quickly.

Remember, there is no such thing as an accredited Masters or Doctorate in hypnosis. The initials R.H. (Registered Hypnotist) or C.M.H. (Certified Master Hypnotist) mean absolutely nothing. Anyone with the proper funds can purchase one of these "degrees" or certifications. Therapists obtain degrees in clinical or counseling psychology; marriage, family and child counseling (MFCC); social work, educational psychology, etc.; not hypnosis.

Always inquire what the letters are after the hypnotherapist's name. A person with no title before his or her name and no letters following has to be doubly ready and willing to answer questions regarding their qualifications to instruct in self-hypnosis. A number of reputable lay hypnotists have compensated for their lack of academic degrees by developing a high level of skill. Those who have supplemented their hypnotic ability with a good knowledge of psychology may be qualified to do this work. Most of this group avoid doing anything along the lines of therapy except under qualified medical supervision; they limit themselves to instructing, to technical problems involving the induction of hypnosis, and to helping in the attainment of social, educational, cultural, and other nontherapeutic aims. It is a deplorable fact that there are many over-enthusiastic, poorly trained hypnotists who will undertake to teach "all comers" the art of self-hypnosis for a fee, assuring the applicant that success is just a matter of willingness on his part (willingness, I suppose, to pay the fee).

Your clinician should be knowledgeable about all aspects of karma and shielding techniques and be able to answer all your questions, offering appropriate guidance as needed. A review of the books on the reading list will provide sufficient background for posing the right kind of questions to your practitioner. If it dawns on you that you know more than the therapist does, it is time to leave immediately.

If past life therapy is part of your treatment, it is crucial that you do not allow unpleasant discoveries to result in feelings of guilt, fear, or resentment. It is almost statistically impossible not to have lived as a murderer, thief, or prostitute at one time, given the hundreds of past lives through which we've all passed. Remember that on balance, most of our past lives have been characterized by honesty, virtue, generosity, and kindness. The therapist should be able to help you defuse any negative revelations, guiding you to the recognition that the purpose of these lives is to allow the soul to grow. This growth requires that life be viewed from many different angles.

When it comes to choosing a therapist, always trust your instincts. If he or she is qualified but you don't like or trust him or her, terminate the relationship. Not only will you not succeed with that particular practitioner, but you might just be susceptible to his or her negative karma.

It is admittedly difficult to direct the prospective patient to a suitable hypnotherapist. In most large metropolitan areas there are ample numbers of these practitioners. Unfortunately, most of them are of questionable ability and reputation. This chapter's purpose is to assist in your search for a clinician.

Be wary of one-shot cures by a prospective hypnotherapist. It is rare that a patient with any significant issue can be treated in less than five sessions. All ethical hypnotherapists should teach self-hypnosis. This discourages dependency on the clinician and encourages empowerment on your part.

Psychiatrists tend to scoff at hypnosis due mostly to prejudice incurred during their training and personal exposure to Hollywood's version of this field. Here are some suggestions for selecting a hypnotherapist:

- Contact the local medical society. They will often have the name of one of their members who uses hypnosis.

- Ask your family physician. He or she may not use hypnosis, but often will be able to provide you with a referral.

- Contact the local psychological association. You are more likely to find one of their members who practices hypnotherapy.

- Scan the shelves of your local bookstores. Very often the author of a book on self-hypnosis can refer you to a colleague in your area.

- Contact the psychology department of your local university or community college. They will often know of someone you can call.

- Ask your friends or family. You would be surprised how many people you know have been to a hypnotherapist. Word-of-mouth referrals are almost always the best type.

Please do not randomly pick a name from the yellow pages of the phone book. This is the last resort; if you must do so, ask the person several questions to make sure you and he or she will be compatible. By all means, keep away from stage hypnotists and those "practitioners" who happen to hit town with a traveling show.

The following questions can be used as models in interviewing your prospective hypnotherapist:

Q: Why can't people consciously recall past lives?

A. Most people's memory comes from their conscious mind proper (ego). It is the subconscious mind we have to tap to elicit past/future memories.

Q: What methods other than hypnosis can help reveal past and future lives?

A: Meditation, spontaneous regressions and progressions, automatic writing, karmic (Vedic) astrological charts, and contacts with masters and guides and one's own higher self in dreams and daydreams.

Q: How can the present population of the world be explained by reincarnation, assuming there are no new souls?

A: The Oversoul concept states that our soul's energy can split and occupy more than one body at a time. Each of these subsouls splits again and occupies additional bodies. This geometric progression accounts for the current world's population of recycled souls.

Q: Does a belief in reincarnation conflict with a belief in God?

A: Absolutely not. The God energy created the universe and our higher selves are but a component of this perfect energy source.

Q: What is the purpose of our karmic cycle?

A: Spiritual growth. We are only here to perfect our soul's energy so that we may ascend to the higher planes and finally to the God plane (heaven, nirvana, *All That Is*).

Q: Do we ever change sex in our karmic cycle?

A: Yes. Although my research shows that approximately seventy-five percent of our lives are lived as the same sex, we must change sex in order to grow spiritually.

Q My life has been a difficult one, doctor. Could it be that I'm just not supposed to be fulfilled this time around?

A: You karmically choose all obstacles as well as assets in this and all of your lives. The new physics demonstrates that we create our own reality. Absolutely everyone has the potential to improve their lives. You are never doomed to a fate of unhappiness.

Q: What is the one true type of soul healing?

A: There is no one true type. There are dozens of methods that will work. No one therapy will work with everyone. Practitioners naturally gravitate to one or more of these types of healing approaches for their own personal reasons.

Q: Do you guarantee that your hypnosis will work?

A: This is a very important question. No ethical practitioner ever makes such a guarantee. If your prospective hypnotherapist does, do not work with him or her.

Q: Who is ultimately responsible for my healing?

A: You, the patient. A hypnotherapist can only train you to access your own higher self and natural healing energies.

By the end of the initial interview, both hypnotherapist and student should have been able to appraise each other and to have obtained a fair estimate of each other's possibilities. Often the beginnings of a good interpersonal relationship are established at this session. Now they are ready to proceed to the next step.

I hope these guidelines will be helpful to you in choosing your hypnotherapist. Ideally, they should help you avoid making a serious mistake. In the event you are already involved with a therapist who is not likely to help you, I trust you will be enabled to cut your losses and move on like the empowered soul you will become.

For those people who feel hypnosis is unscientific and scoffed at by the medical profession, I have summarized reports by the British and American Medial Associations.

The British report is published in the *Supplement to the British Medical Journal* for April 23, 1955. The British Committee found:

1. There was a great deal of criticism and skepticism from medical societies directed toward those who first practiced hypnosis in Britain. This arose from the use of hypnosis for entertainment, and also exaggerated the claims of its medical effectiveness. The Committee deplores the use of hypnosis for entertainment.

2. The Committee finds that hypnosis is of value in the treatment of psychosomatic disorders and psychoneuroses.

3. It was also determined that hypnoanesthesia has a place for surgical, dental and obstetrical purposes.

4. Hypnosis should only be used within the competence of the practitioner.

5. A knowledge of hypnosis should be given to medical undergraduates during their psychiatric course.

6. Further research in the field is greatly needed and desired.

The report of the American Committee is in the *Journal of the American Medical Association* for September 13, 1958, Vol. 168, No. 2. The Committee finds that:

1. There are proper uses of hypnosis in the hands of properly trained physicians and dentists.

2. Each practitioner should use hypnosis only within his own area of competence.

3. There is a severe lack of training facilities for hypnosis in the United States; such training should be established under the auspices of universities.

4. The use of hypnosis for entertainment is condemned.

5. One member of the Committee took the position that there are dangers in the use of hypnosis, but other consultants were unable to support this position.

6. More research is needed to further delineate the usefulness of hypnosis.

■ ■ ■

APPENDIX

ESTABLISHING A NEW AGE HYPNOTHERAPY PRACTICE

O bviously, the first requirement for becoming a hypnotherapist is to obtain proper training in hypnosis. This workbook may be all that you require, but a comprehensive orientation to hypnosis is always desirable. There are a number of hypnosis schools that will train anyone in the art and science of hypnosis, so a professional degree is not required. My recommendation, however, is to obtain at least a Masters Degree in clinical or counseling psychology, social work, or an M.F.C.C. (or equivalent degree).

When you have obtained sufficient training and are ready to devote yourself to establishing a practice, you will need to decide various issues. First check the yellow pages of your local telephone directory to locate other hypnotists in the area. Talk to them and obtain their feedback as to the climate in the community. Mention your specialty, as they may act as a referral source for "unusual" cases they do not want to treat.

Check the legal requirements in your community. Some regions require a business license. Consult an attorney to make sure you are not in violation of any state or local ordinance.

Part-time vs. Full-time practice

Relatively few practitioners begin full-time operation immediately. You may decide to start a few evenings each week and have weekend appointments. This can be expanded as your practice grows. I do not advise quitting your regular job before you have established your New Age hypnotherapy practice.

If your decision is to go into hypnosis full time, it would be wise to have sufficient financial resources to enable you to live for six months to a year. If your financial resources do not warrant this kind of an arrangement, beginning with a part-time operation is probably necessary. Either way, I recommend sending out announcements to the community and the local media prior to opening your doors to the public.

OFFICE SET-UP

Please refer back to chapter 3 for recommendations for setting up the therapy room you will use to see clients. Hypnotic aids are also discussed in that chapter that will assist you in conducting and marketing your New Age hypnotherapy practice.

At least two rooms are required for the practice of hypnosis—a waiting room and a consulting or induction room. Even though your practice is by appointment only, a client may show up too early, so a comfortable place to wait should be provided. Many hypnotists have three-room set-ups consisting of a waiting room, a consulting room, and an induction room; the consulting room is used for the interview and pre-hypnotic discussions, while the induction room is used for the actual induction of hypnosis and related work.

All the rooms should be dignified and tasteful in decor, reflecting a professional environment. It is quite acceptable to have a selection of hypno-aids in evidence, but there should not be any appearance of a display of gimmickry.

You do not need a soundproof room for inductions, but it should be free of disturbing influences. This room should be separately furnished and be at least 10 by 12 feet. I highly recommend a recliner for the client; you may elect to also include a couch so your subject can be given a choice.

Make sure there is proper circulation of air in this room. The lighting should be adjustable in intensity and subdued. Bookcases holding your library of reference books and hypnotic aids will set a confidence-inspiring tone. If there is a telephone in the induction room, make sure it can be switched off so there will be no sudden jarring interruption of the induction process. The sound of a telephone coming from an adjoining room, however, is not necessarily disturbing, particularly if the operator attaches no importance to it when it rings.

Working Under a Trade Name or As an Individual

This is strictly a matter of choice. A hypnotist who is well known would probably be better off working under his own name. However, when a person first starts out, it might be advisable to work under a trade name. Trade names should be registered with the appropriate government agency and copies of the registration should be available for banks, post offices, and other institutions that may require evidence of name registration. The bank, for instance, will usually refuse to permit a depositor to open a business account under a trade name or to cash checks issued to a trade name unless that name has been duly registered.

In registering a trade name, it is necessary to check business names already registered to make sure that you don't use someone else's name. This could result in lawsuits for infringement. Hypnotists sometimes use designations such such as "Center" or "Institute." The designation of "School" should be avoided. In most states, to register a trade name with the word "school" in it may require clearance with the State Department of Education. This department will usually refuse approval to any venture with the word "school" in it unless one conforms to all of the requirements of setting up an educational institution.

One thing you must be extremely cautious about is not using in your trade name a word or phrase that has a medical connotation. Such words as "clinic" are taboo. Anything with the word "medical" or the word "psychological" in it should likewise be avoided. Such terminology has strong implications and might lead the public to assume that the trade name covers some form of medical practice. Of course, these precautions aren't necessary if you are a licensed physician or psychotherapist.

Registration vs. Incorporation
Your attorney should also be consulted on whether the trade name should be registered by you as an individual or whether it might be advisable to incorporate your operation. There are considerations both pro and con in connection with incorporation. Your own personal situation, your financial condition, and other matters should be taken into account when deciding this important question.

Insurance
A liability policy for your office is highly recommended. You can obtain malpractice insurance by joining the National Guild of Hypnotists.

Certification
The N.G.H. and the A.I.H. (see chapter 3) have certification programs. Certification by these organizations lends prestige to your operation.

Advertising

A small listing in the yellow pages of the local telephone directory will serve you well; large, glaring ads appear unprofessional. No claims or guarantees should be included in your advertising. Many hypnotists use the phrase, "Instruction in Hypnosis and Self-Hypnosis" and then leave it to the inquirer to obtain details on specific problems when he or she calls. There is nothing wrong in stating that you do past life regressions.

SOURCES OF CLIENTS

Contact local physicians, psychologists, and counselors and send them a brochure and your card to solicit professional referrals. In addition to the hypnotist contact I mentioned earlier, this is an excellent source of quality clients.

Immediately after your first session with a new client, write to the referring doctor, thanking him or her, and offer to keep them informed of the client's progress.

This letter will help establish a professional relationship. You need not go into details of a past life regression or superconscious mind tap, unless the referring professional is specifically interested in this field and the client has given you permission to discuss his or her case. Be sure to keep a copy of this letter.

If, after interviewing the client the first time, you find that there are related problems that are not within the scope of your practice, do not hesitate to phone or write the referring doctor and explain what you found. He or she will give you credit for your perceptiveness and your caution. If you feel that the client needs psychological or psychiatric treatment, do not make the mistake of yourself referring that person to a psychologist or psychiatrist. Get in touch with the doctor and suggest that he or she do it, or if they don't know of anyone, you might give the doctor a couple of names to whom he or she can make the appropriate referral. No doctor will think less of you when you admit that a certain case is "over your head" or not within your area of competence.

All correspondence with the referring professional should be neatly typewritten, with proper spelling, grammar, and sentence construction; until the doctor knows you personally, your correspondence will reflect your image. I am using the term "doctor" here to illustrate a principle. Your referring licensed professional may not be a doctor. In that case, use the appropriate title in your correspondence.

Adult School Courses

Several sources of these programs are available in your community. Community colleges are one example. Check with your local library for others. During such courses, the nature of your own work can be explained and this, too, will result in inquiries.

Lecture-Demonstrations

One of the best ways to get started is to offer your services to local civic, fraternal, social, and educational groups. Even without offering your service, the mere fact that you have set up a practice and have announced it will usually inspire the Lions Club, the Kiwanis Club, and other organizations to contact you for lectures. During these lectures, you can of course mention the various areas of applications of hypnosis, including the New Age approach you take. This usually will result in inquiries from listeners.

In addition to the lecture, it is also advisable to give a low-key demonstration. Such demonstrations must not resemble the stage shows with which most people are familiar. They must be strictly educational and must be conducted on a dignified level. Anything glaring or spectacular will put you in the wrong light. I use videotapes of past television interviews in my seminars and workshops. The audience will immediately identify with the show and I can control the amount of time it takes to demonstrate my techniques.

Your own client referrals are by far the best source of additional clients. People who are satisfied with professional services inform their friends, family, and co-workers of this fact.

CASSETTE TAPES

There is no more efficient method of teaching self-hypnosis than by the use of tapes. You can record a standard conditioning tape using your own induction and technique. Not only will your client work better and faster this way, but he or she may share this tape with others and speak kindly of you in the process.

These tapes will pay off with great karmic dividends in the future. They are inexpensive to produce; sources of equipment and supplies for manufacturing your own hypnosis tapes are listed at the end of this chapter, and you are welcome to contact my office for a comprehensive list of professional recorded audio and videotapes for training and your own experimental use.

The following script is taken from the induction on the tapes I distribute to my patients:

Standard Induction for All Tapes

(Ocean sound alone for about ten seconds, then metronome beats in the back in sync to my voice.)

- Sit back and listen to the beats of the metronome in
- the background. Each beat of the metronome will
- take you deeper and deeper into relaxation. Listen as
- I count backward from 20 to 1. Each count back-
- ward will make each and every muscle in your body
- more completely relaxed until I reach the count of 1
- in which you will be in a very deep and relaxed level
- of hypnosis. 20, 19, 18, deeply, deep relaxed. 17, 16,
- 15, down, down, down. 14, 13, 12, very, very deep.

- 11, 10, 9, deep, deep relaxed. 8, 7, 6, so very sleepy.
- 5, 4, 3, deep, deeply relaxed. 2, 1, deep, deep asleep.
- 20, 20, 20. You are now in a deeply relaxed level of hypnosis. Listen as I count backward, again this time from 7 to 1. As I count backward from 7 to 1, you are going to hear the beats of the metronome in the background decrease in volume, decrease in volume with each count until I reach the count of 1, in which you will hear nothing but my voice. You will be in a very, very deep and relaxed level of hypnosis.

- Decease metronome beats until the count of 1, when they are gone completely. 7, deeper, deeper, deeper, down, down. down. 6, deeper, deeper, deeper, down, down, down. 5, deeper, deeper, deeper, down, down, down. 4, deeper, deeper, deeper, down, down, down. 3, deeper, deeper, deeper, down, down, down. 2, deeper, deeper, deeper, down, down, down. 1, deeply, deeply relaxed, deeply, deeply asleep. 20, 20, 20. You are now in a nice deep relaxed level of hypnosis. The repetition of the number 20 three times in succession by your voice will quickly and very deeply get you into this nice deep level of hypnosis. This will get you quicker and deeper each and every time you practice self-hypnosis.

You can add whatever instructions you want to from this point on and end the trance as follows:

- Now, in a few moments...when I count up to 5... you will open your eyes and be wide awake again. You will feel much better for this deep, refreshing sleep. You will feel completely relaxed...both mentally and

- physically...quite calm and composed...without the
- slightest feeling of drowsiness or tiredness.

- And next time...you will not only be able to go into
- this sleep much more quickly and easily...but you
- will be able to go much more deeply.

One...two...three...four...five...wide awake and
refreshed.

THE PRE-HYPNOSIS DISCUSSION

One of the best methods to allay fears of hypnosis and to establish a professional relationship with a client is to conduct an informative "pre-hypnosis talk." The following paragraphs summarize the major points I cover in this dialogue.

I begin by asking the patient what he or she knows or has heard about hypnosis, and what he or she expects to happen during and after the hypnotic state. Most of the patients' ideas about this discipline have been derived from newspaper articles, sensational magazine stories, stage performances, movies, or television. They expect to be completely unconscious during the period of the trance, and to remember nothing at all of what has happened once the trance has ended.

I tell them that there is no real resemblance between hypnotic sleep and ordinary sleep. Although during the induction their eyes will begin to feel more and more tired and will close just as they do when they go to sleep, yet all the while their eyes are closed they will remain just as wide awake and alert as when their eyes were open.

I tell the patient that he or she need not necessarily expect to forget what has happened during the trance once it has passed. Since the patient has probably seen demonstrations of hypnotic experiments on television, in which specially trained subjects are used, he will often get the idea that exactly the same things are going to happen to him if he allows himself to be hypnotized. Most important is the fact that he will certainly expect to have a complete loss of memory for what has occurred during the trance state, and when he finds that he remembers everything that has happened he will be convinced that he has never actually been hypnotized at all. Consequently, if you fail to correct his views on these points, particularly regarding his anticipated loss of memory, you will encounter exactly the same skepticism that we have just discussed and a similar result will be inevitable. I usually tell the patient that few people are able to achieve such depth, and that for ordinary clinical purposes it is certainly not necessary and very seldom desirable.

I explain to the patient that although will power is most important in the induction of hypnosis, it is in fact his own will power that plays a significant part and not that of the hypnotist. There is a widespread impression among the general public that if you allow yourself to be hypnotized, you have no choice but to obey implicitly all the hypnotist's commands—that it is his greater will power that causes you to surrender yours completely, with the result that you are bound to carry out his orders automatically. This, of course, links up the next difficulty on our list—the fear of being dominated—with the fear of losing control, which has already been mentioned.

I tell the patient that if we really believed this to be true, I don't think many of us would be willing to allow ourselves to be hypnotized. I know that I wouldn't. If hypnosis could only be produced through the stronger will power of the hypnotist, it would naturally follow that the easiest people to hypnotize would be very weak-willed people. This is certainly not the case, for in actual fact the reverse happens to be true.

I assure the patient that he need have no fear whatsoever of being dominated by the hypnotist, and that he can never be compelled to do or say anything to which he strongly objects. I explain that if one were to try to compel him to do such a thing, it would arouse so much mental conflict in his mind (I must, but I can't) that he would come out of trance by himself immediately.

I am quite honest with him and tell him that if he allows me to induce a really deep trance state, there is no doubt that he will feel impelled to carry out my instructions implicitly, but only insofar as he is prepared to do so and yield authority temporarily to me. I am unable to compel him to do anything that would be in violation of his moral or ethical code.

The "power" of hypnosis is a power of the person being hypnotized, NOT the "power" of the hypnotist. Words have power in that they produce ideas in the minds of the listeners. The acceptance of certain ideas constitutes hypnosis.

Anyone who can speak and read with reasonable freedom can induce hypnosis. Almost anyone can respond to hypnotic suggestion, to a greater or lesser degree after a period of training. Suggestion of the "hypnotic" type plays a great part in our everyday lives. We are constantly exposed to it, and it can be used deliberately and purposefully for our physical and emotional benefit.

I instruct the patient NOT TO TRY too hard, but be relaxed. A vigorous effort to *be* hypnotized will prevent a good response as much as a strong resistance.

I describe what would occur if I died while the patient was in trance. Don't laugh, this is a very common question. The reaction of a subject to the sudden disappearance of the hypnotist would vary with depth of the trance and type of condition. A light-trance subject can almost literally awaken at will. A patient in a somnambulistic (deep) trance would either come out of the hypnosis in a short time or go into a natural sleep and be out of the trance when he awakened from the sleep.

I finally say to the patient: "I really do not hypnotize you, and I have never hypnotized a single human being in my life! However, *many individuals have entered into deep hypnosis because they really wanted to do so.* I cannot make you close your eyes by suggesting eye closure unless you wish to close your eyes. I cannot make you count to yourself if you do not wish to count. And I have no way of knowing whether or not you are counting to yourself. I cannot make you lift your arm, can I, if you do not care to lift it? Our relationship, therefore, is a co-operative one and *not* a mental 'tug of war.'"

Many of these preliminary explanations, however, can be dispensed with in the case of children who, unless excessively timid and nervous, are usually much more easily hypnotized than adults. Children are much less critical and are usually much more amenable to persuasion and suggestion. Here one can rely almost entirely on the "prestige factor" combined with a sympathetic and understanding approach.

I generally tell young children that I would like to teach them how to go into a special kind of sleep—that although their eyes will begin to feel tired and will close exactly as they do when they go to sleep at night, it will be quite different because they will be able to hear everything that I say, and will even be able to talk to me without waking up. Provided that I have already gained the child's confidence and succeed in arousing his or her interest, I find that this is usually all that is required.

The time spent in removing misconceptions, doubts, and fears is never wasted. It will not only ensure more rapid and successful inductions, but failure will become much less frequent. When I have completed my explanations to patients, I always ask them whether they have any other questions for me. By answering them, I am usually able to dispel any last lingering doubts and fears, thus securing their full cooperation and trust. I let them see quite clearly that hypnosis is essentially a matter of teamwork between the doctor and the patient. That the part they play, however passive it may be, is every bit as important as mine, and that without their cooperation and willingness nothing can be achieved.

OVERCOMING RESISTANCE

Whenever difficulty occurs, it is important to discover the nature of the difficulty. It may be that the technique you have adopted will have to be modified to suit the needs of this particular subject, but even this cannot properly be decided until the nature of the difficulty is known. The best approach is to question the subject closely as to the precise sensations experienced during the induction, and any difficulties that were felt. The following sections discuss common causes of subject resistance to hypnosis.

Over-anxiety and Fear of Failure.

This is a very common source of difficulty. Over-anxiety to succeed with hypnosis is almost bound to interfere with successful induction. It is nearly always present to some extent in the subject who seeks psychological help and advice. To deal with this situation, give the subject the strongest possible reassurance and encouragement before proceeding with further attempts at induction.

Fear of the Hypnotic State Itself

It sometimes happens that while the subject may be consciously anxious and willing to be hypnotized, the patient may also be subconsciously afraid of succumbing to the trance. When this is so, his or her subconscious fear is usually that of "losing control," and the mental conflict that consequently arises is quite sufficient to prevent them from entering the hypnotic state at all.

Give the subject the reassurance required regarding their fears, and also promise that nothing will be done without their prior knowledge and consent. Stress the fact that it will be impossible to obtain any effect that they are unwilling to produce.

Inadequate Preparation before Induction

Most of the difficulties encountered in trance induction will be greatly lessened, if not entirely removed, if the subject's mind has been fully prepared before any attempt is made. A review of the pre-induction discussion will illustrate a proper preparation of the subject for hypnosis.

Defiance of Authority

Sometimes a subject will admit the fact that, during the induction of hypnosis, he or she experiences an irresistible impulse to oppose everything that is being suggested. You should point out to them that hypnosis is essentially a matter of teamwork, that without his or her full cooperation nothing can be achieved and that you seek to exercise no more authority over him or her than they are willing to grant in order to treat the condition successfully.

Fluctuation of Attention

This usually occurs in subjects who have what is aptly called a "grasshopper" mind. Their powers of concentration are poor, and their minds cannot remain fixed upon one idea, or their attention held for long enough to permit the induction to be successful. Their minds flit incessantly from one topic to another.

The best way of dealing with this, by far, is to use a modified counting technique. The following method is the one that I have found to be most satisfactory:

I want you to start counting slowly, to yourself... and to go on counting until you hear me tell you to stop.

When you say...one...Close your eyes!

When you say...two...Open your eyes!

When you say...three...Close your eyes!

When you say...four...Open your eyes.

As the subject counts to him- or herself, they open and shut their eyes deliberately with each alternate count. While they are doing this they are quietly told how sleepy they are becoming, that their eyes are becoming more and more tired and their eyelids heavier and heavier, that presently their eyes will want to remain closed and they will fall into a deep, deep sleep.

Need to Prove Superiority

In dealing with such subjects, it is necessary to emphasize the importance of the part that they themselves play in the actual induction of hypnosis. At the same time, every possible step should be taken to increase their motivation and pride of achievement. You should tell them that it is only very intelligent people who make good hypnotic subjects, since a considerable degree of concentration and cooperation is required.

Physical Discomfort

Physical discomfort can greatly hinder the successful induction of hypnosis; therefore the subject should be made as comfortable as possible. He or she should visit the bathroom before settling down on the couch or chair. Drafts should be avoided, and the subject should be kept warm. Loud or unexpected noises should be avoided.

Dislike of the Method Employed

Sometimes a subject dislikes the method of induction or may dislike something in the actual phrasing of your suggestions. For instance, some subjects object to the word "sleepy." If so, you should discard that word and substitute the words "tiredness" or "drowsiness" only, during the next induction. Similarly, when the phrase "you are sinking into a deeper, deeper sleep" has been used, a subject has been known to complain that upon the word sinking, he or she invariably experienced a most uncomfortable sinking sensation in the pit of the stomach. In this case, the mere substitution of the word "falling" will be quite sufficient to remove this discomfort, and also reassure the subject that nothing will be forced upon him. Whenever it is the actual induction method that the subject dislikes, you should always adopt an alternative procedure at your next attempt at induction.

Lack of Motivation

Those who have little or no desire to get well are poor subjects for hypnosis. It is almost impossible to induce hypnosis unless the subject is sufficiently motivated. Many subjects, such as alcoholics, smokers, and overeaters, do not wish to yield their symptoms because they have a "self-defeating sequence" mentality.

PUBLICITY

The electronic and print media can be very helpful in assisting your practice's growth. I will devote the rest of this chapter to instructions on how you can obtain this free publicity. Although most of this material deals with radio and television, you can modify this approach to the print media.

The Press Kit

A professional press kit is simply a collection of background information about yourself and something that you are trying to promote (a book, workshop, etc.). The contents of this kit will vary depending on what you are trying to sell. The following items are usually included in a press kit:

1. Press releases.

2. Biography sheet.

3. Photograph.

4. Copies of print articles written about you.

5. Your office brochure.

6. Business card.

7. Videotapes and/or audiotapes.

These items should be accompanied by a cover memo or letter that is tailored to the particular media niche you are approaching. A sample memo from my own press kit is shown on page 210 to give you an idea of the type of information useful to a producer.

How to Get on Radio and Television Talk Shows

You must know what exposure you want and be willing to work with media personnel to meet their needs in order to obtain interviews. The main concern of the electronic media is ratings, not promoting you or your services. Look at your pitch from their perspective; if you come up with an exciting angle, you are well on your way to being scheduled as a guest on a talk show.

New Age topics are always popular with the audience, but many producers take a dim view of the field. The burden is on you to create an angle that will convince even the skeptic to book you on the show. An interesting angle, especially if you can tie it into a current trend or news story, will increase your chances of success. Examples of good angles are past lives experiences as explanation for overweight individuals; how to increase your psychic ability; how to do self-hypnosis; how to resolve relationship problems through past life regression, etc.

Your Telephone Call to the Media

Your local station affiliate can help you with providing the talk show and producers telephone numbers. When you speak to a producer, first establish your topic and your credentials. Next, develop your angle for the show. You must be prepared as you won't have much time to sell your idea to him or her.

The best time to make this initial call is early in the morning. The producer will advise you of a better time to call if this is not convenient to them. Send your press kit out immediately and follow up from seven to ten days later with another call.

When you phone the producer again, make sure you are fully prepared to reiterate your angle; keep notes available if necessary.

Re: Dr. Bruce Goldberg
Past Life Regression/Future Life Progression

Enclosed you will find material on my work using hypnosis to regress patients into past lives and progress them into future lifetimes. Also enclosed is a VHS of actual people going through these experiences; a copy of my book, The Search for Grace, which was made into a movie and aired on May 17, 1994; and a copy of my award-winning book, Soul Healing. My previous book, Past Lives—Future Lives, was the first book ever written on progression therapy. I would very much like to demonstrate these techniques on your show. The enclosed tapes of a KABC and KFI radio interviews include live regressions and progressions of the hosts.

For thirteen years I was a practicing dentist using hypnosis on my dental patients. While using hypnosis to relax my patients, I began regressing them into past lives. This sideline evolved into a full-time profession as my reputation spread. I gave up my dental practice to become the only full-time hypnotherapist who specializes in past life regression and future life progression (that's correct, I progress patients into their future lives!). I have conducted over 33,000 regressions and progressions on over 11,000 patients since 1974 and have helped thousands of people rid themselves of phobias, habits, negative tendencies, etc. I practice in Los Angeles.

Please review the enclosed material. I will take the liberty of following up this correspondence with a telephone call to discuss the possibilities. Thank you for your consideration.

Sincerely,
Bruce Goldberg, D.D.S., M.S.
BG/al
Enclosures

If your contact requests any additional information, send it immediately.

Always be cooperative and professional. Press kits and books are sometimes misplaced or discarded, so you may be asked to resubmit your materials. If the producer senses that you are demanding or too insecure, they will quickly lose interest in you.

There are three types of responses the producer may express:

- I liked the idea, but it isn't right for our show.

- The topic doesn't appeal to me at all.

- Your idea is great. Let's talk about scheduling an interview.

When the producer tells you what he or she didn't like, it is now up to you to redesign your approach to meet their needs. For example, I spoke to a radio producer about using the topic of past life causes of overeating. My case summary included a woman who starved to death in the Sahara Desert during an Egyptian past life. The producer liked the past life angle but felt that the "starved to death" cause was overdone, so I substituted another case of an overweight female patient (Evelyn) who constantly disappointed men in her relationships. The producer loved this case and he scheduled me for a three-hour interview on a nationally syndicated radio show.

If the producer simply doesn't like the topic, thank them for their time and politely end the conversation. You can suggest a different angle if it's merely your approach that the producer didn't like.

If the producer likes your pitch or idea, you are ready to work out a time and date for the interview. When you are booked as a guest, make sure you obtain the following information from the producer:

1. Is the show live or taped? How long is your segment?

2. Find out what the theme of the show is that particular day.

3. Will you be part of a panel? If the answer to this is yes, find out who the other guests are. Read background material (books, articles, etc.) on the other guests as part of your preparation for the interview.

4. Check travel arrangements and directions to the studio. Confirm your arrival time at the studio.

Thank the host and producer for the interview and follow up with a short note. This is part of your networking, as it is desirable to "reincarnate" on these shows as your career progresses. It is always easier to book a second interview, assuming your first interview was well received.

A FINAL WORD ABOUT YOUR NEW AGE HYPNOTHERAPY CAREER CHOICE

To fulfill your karmic purpose in this endeavor, let me suggest the following guidelines:

1. Do daily superconscious mind taps and visualize yourself achieving specific goals.

2. Totally dedicate yourself to preparing and executing this career decision.

3. Work out any "self-defeating sequences" you may have and always "practice what you preach."

4. Do your very best to surround yourself with positive, spiritually evolved souls who are the best at what they do.

For those people who may criticize your choice of a career, you may quote from the Tibetans: "*Sabbadanam dhammadanam jinati*": "The best of all gifts is the gift of Truth."

RESOURCES

National Cassette Systems, Inc.
613 N. Commerce Avenue
P.O. Box 99
Front Royal, VA 22630
(800) 541–0551

This is an excellent source for blank cassettes, vinyl albums, art services for J-cards, studio services and duplication of audio and video tapes.

Martel Electronics
Placentia Business Center
2013 Miraloma
Placentia, CA 92670

This company distributes the Telex Copyette 1- & 3-cassette copier. You can duplicate three sixty-minute cassettes in two minutes. Both sides of the tape are duplicated. It takes only three minutes to duplicate a ninety-minute tape.

Media Directories

These are expensive but worth the money in the long run.

Public Relations Plus, Inc.
P.O. Box 1197
New Milford, CT 06776
(800) 999–8448

Morgan-Rand Publishing Company
2200 Sansom Street
Philadelphia, PA 19103
(215) 557–8200

Publishes *TV and Cable Publicity Outlets* and other books.

Broadcast Interview Source
2233 Wisconsin Avenue N.W.
Washington, D.C. 20007–4112
Publishes *Talk Show Selects* and other books.

Mailing Lists

Direct Mail List Rates and Data
5201 Old Orchard Road
Skokie, IL 60076

Publicity Books

Hannaford, Peter. *Talking Back to the Media*. New York: Facts on File Publications, 1986.

Parinello, Al. *On the Air*. Hawthorne, New Jersey: The Career Press, 1991.

Pinskey, Raleigh. *The Zen of Hype*. New York: Citadel Press, 1991.

Other books:

Walters, Dottie and Lilly Walters. *Speak and Grow Rich*. Englewood Cliffs, New Jersey: Prentice Hall, 1989.

Maggio, Rosalie. *How to Say It*. Englewood Cliffs, New Jersey: Prentice Hall, 1990.

Tarila, Sophia. *New Marketing Opportunities*. Sedona, Arizona: First Editions, 1995.

GLOSSARY
OF TERMS

Age progression: The guiding of a subject into the future of their current life.

Age regression: By suggestion, a subject is caused to revert to an earlier age in this life.

Akashic records: The compilation of all of our past, present, and future lives, reportedly stored on the causal plane.

Amnesia: By suggestion, certain items are blocked temporarily from memory.

Autogenic training: A term devised by J. H. Schultz of Germany. It consists of a series of mental exercises to produce relaxation; probably related to autohypnosis.

Autohypnosis: a self-induced state of hypnosis.

Automatic writing or drawing: The hand moves autonomously without conscious guidance by the subject. This was the first proof of the existence of the subconscious.

Cancel: Any suggestion given in the hypnotic trance which the therapist does not wish to carry over into the non-trance state should be canceled. For example, if the subject has developed glove anesthesia which should be terminated with the hypnotic trance, then the hypnotist should say: "Your hand will now have its normal feeling."

Cleansing: The process of introducing the subconscious mind (soul) to the superconscious mind (higher self) for the purpose of raising the soul's frequency vibrational rate to a higher level. This results in spiritual growth along with the permanent elimination of self-defeating sequences (SDS).

Complaint: A substitute term for the word "symptom."

Counter-suggestion: If a suggestion is given which is not accepted by the subject, it acts as a counter-suggestion, i.e., it will be more difficult for the subject to accept subsequent suggestions.

Cue: In giving post-hypnotic suggestions, a signal (cue) is usually provided as part of the suggestion. When this cue is given, the suggestion is to be carried out. A cue is also often used to terminate a post-hypnotic suggestion.

Deepening methods: Methods that are designed to help a subject go into a deeper level of hypnosis.

Defense mechanism: The ego or beta brain wave. These components of our conscious mind proper try to prevent changes (spiritual growth) in our behavior. Rationalization, intellectualization, displacement and sublimation are some examples.

Dehypnotizing: Helping the subject to come out of the hypnotic trance.

Depth of hypnosis: Different levels of hypnosis with varying degrees of physiological and psychological characteristics. The simplest breakdown is light, medium, and deep.

Direct suggestion: An idea presented directly to the subject with the hope that he will accept it uncritically and wholeheartedly. Most of the suggestions used in the induction techniques are direct suggestions.

Disassociation: A splitting of one part of the personality from another. May be produced in some subjects by hypnotic suggestions, e.g., the subject sitting in this chair sees himself in the chair across the room. Examples of a lesser degree of disassociation are found in successful levitation suggestions.

Double-bind: A subject is given a choice of alternatives, either of which leads to a desired result. This has the aspect of permissiveness and the subject finds it difficult to avoid making a choice, but the choice commits him to a course of action. Simple example: Speaking to a young child: "Would you rather go to bed now or in ten minutes?"

Empowerment: The principle of taking charge of your life (and future lifetimes) by using cleansing techniques.

Fractionating method: A method designed to deepen hypnosis. It consists of alternately going in and out of hypnosis. Sometimes the subject is questioned when out of hypnosis concerning his feelings while in the trance. This information is then fed back to him in the next trance.

Frequency: A parallel universe in a past, present, or future life.

Glove anesthesia: Analgesia of the hand to the wrist.

Group hypnosis: The use of an induction technique with a group instead of a single individual.

Hand levitation: The lifting of the hand in an involuntary manner.

Heterohypnosis: A state of hypnosis in which the subject is guided into the alpha state by another person.

Higher self: The perfect part of our soul's energy—also known as the superconscious mind. The soul merges with this when it is perfect and ascends to the higher planes.

Hypnosis: The natural alpha level characterized by focused concentration, creativity, and relaxation. Daydreams are examples of this state.

Hypnotherapist: A hypnotist with academic credentials in medicine or psychology.

Hypnotic suggestion: A suggestion given while the subject is in the hypnotic state; to be carried out while still in hypnosis.

Hypnotist: One who helps another to go into the hypnotic state. An alternate term is Operator. This usually connotes a person without professional credentials.

Hypnotizability: The ability of the subject to go into the hypnotic state or trance.

Karma: A cause and effect principle that states that the soul will not be able to ascend beyond the lower five planes (karmic cycle) until it has perfected its energy.

Masters and guides: These perfect souls are not us, but assist us in our spiritual growth. Some people refer to them as angels.

Near-death experience: A type of out-of-body experience during which the physical body clinically dies for a short period of time.

Negative hallucination: The subject fails to sense something that is quite obvious.

Negative suggestion: A suggestion stated negatively, e.g., "This won't hurt." As a rule, suggestions stated negatively are less effective than positive suggestions.

Out-of-body experience: An altered state of consciousness during which the astral body leaves the physical body. This occurs naturally during all dream states.

Parallel universe: A universe identical to ours, but existing on a different frequency in the same place and time as our world. "Parallel life" is the term for the incarnation on this frequency.

Past life regression: Guiding a subject back to a prior lifetime with hypnosis or other means.

Plane: A dimension of the universe. There are reportedly five lower planes that make up the karmic cycle; a soul plane (where the subconscious chooses its next life), and seven higher planes (the highest plane being the God plane, nirvana, *All That Is*, etc.).

Positive hallucination: By suggestion the subject has a sensory experience of something that does not exist.

Positive suggestion: A suggestion stated in a positive manner, e.g., "Please sit down," versus "Please do not stand."

Posthypnotic suggestion: A suggestion given during the hypnotic trance but which is to be carried out after the termination of the hypnotic state. This is a very helpful device for therapy.

Quantum mechanics: Also known as quantum physics or the new physics. This hard science studies the behavior of matter and energy at the level of atoms and subatomic particles.

Rapport: A subject in hypnosis will often respond to the hypnotist only; then the subject is said to be in rapport with the hypnotist.

Rehypnotizing: Helping a subject go back into a state of hypnosis. Usually this involves the use of a posthypnotic suggestion.

Resistance: Some individuals have difficulty going into hypnosis, possibly because of erroneous ideas concerning hypnosis or from other causes. Resistances may be conscious; i.e., subject to verbalization; or subconscious, not subject to verbalization at the moment.

Revivication: The subject relives, with a feeling of present reality, a previous or future experience. These experiences usually have a strong emotional component.

Self-defeating sequences (SDS): These are defense mechanisms (ego) techniques to prevent the soul from growing spiritually. Procrastination, habits, and phobias are examples of this. Cleansing techniques help to permanently eliminate these by raising the quality of the soul's energy.

Soul: This is the subconscious mind or spirit. It is an imperfect form of our alpha brain-wave state that is trapped in the karmic cycle until it is perfected.

Soulmate: Another subconscious mind manifested in a physical body that has shared many lives with us. This class is further subdivided into true soulmates, boundary soulmates, and retribution soulmates.

Soul plane ascension: The process of the soul merging with its higher self and rising to the higher planes. This can only be accomplished when the soul is perfect. Cleansing techniques facilitate this process.

Space-time continuum: The quantum physics concept that states all time (past, present, and future) is simultaneous. We are thus living all of our lives now.

Suggestion: An idea that is presented so that it is accepted by the subject with a minimum of analysis, criticism and resistance. This idea will lead to or modify behavior.

Superconscious mind: The higher self or perfect energy representation of the soul. This energy comes directly from the God plane. This mind advises the soul during the dream state (REM cycle) and sometimes during the waking day in the form of insights and psychic (ESP) experiences.

Symptom: Besides the ordinary use of this term in medicine and dentistry, it is used in psychotherapy to apply to the complaint that the subject presents.

Trance: A term used to describe the hypnotic experience. The word "state" may be used instead.

Uncertainty principle: Also referred to as the principle of indeterminism. This concept states that it is impossible to predict the future based on the past or present. Werner Heisenberg, during the 1920s, developed this principle by proving that we cannot know with absolute certainty both the position and path of a particle.

Unconscious mind: The part of our mind that is unaware and unawake. The theta and delta brain waves represent this sleep state. Freud incorrectly used this term to describe the subconscious mind.

BIBLIOGRAPHY

Bernstein, M. *The Search for Bridey Murphy.* New York: Doubleday, 1956.

Burnham, Sophy. *A Book of Angels: Reflections on Angels Past & Present & True Stories of How They Touch Our Lives.* New York: Ballantine, 1990.

Cheek, D. B., and L. LeCron. *Clinical Hypnotherapy.* New York: Grune & Stratton, 1968.

Ebon, M. *The Signet Handbook of Parapsychology.* New York: Signet, 1978.

Erickson, M. E. and E. L. Rossi. *Experiencing Hypnosis: Therapeutic Approaches to Altered States.* New York: Irvington Publishers, 1981.

Fowler, R. *The Watchers.* New York: Bantam, 1990.

Gardner, G. G., and K. Olness. *Hypnosis and Hypnotherapy with Children.* Orlando: Grune & Stratton, 1981.

Goldberg, Bruce. *Soul Healing.* St. Paul: Llewellyn Publications, 1997.

———. *The Search for Grace: The True Story of Murder and Reincarnation.* St. Paul: Llewellyn Publications, 1997.

———. *Past Lives—Future Lives.* New York: Ballantine Books, 1988.

———. "Slowing Down the Aging Process through the Use of Altered States of Consciousness: A Review of the Medical Literature." *Psychology: A Journal of Human Behavior,* 1995, 32(2), 19–22.

———. "Regression and Progression in Past Life Therapy." *National Guild of Hypnotists Newsletter,* 1994, Jan./Feb., 1, 10.

———. "Quantum Physics and Its Application to Past Life Regression and Future Life Progression Hypnotherapy." *Journal of Regression Therapy,* 1993, 7(1), 89–93.

———. "Depression: A Past Life Cause." *National Guild of Hypnotists Newsletter,* 1993, Oct./Nov., 7, 14.

———. "The Clinical Use of Hypnotic Regression and Progression in Hypnotherapy." *Psychology: A Journal of Human Behavior,* 1990, 27(1), 43–48.

———. "Your Problem May Come from Your Future: A Case Study." *Journal of Regression Therapy,* 1990, 4(2), 21–29.

———. "The Treatment of Cancer through Hypnosis." *Psychology: A Journal of Human Behavior,* 1985, 3(4), 36–39.

———. "Hypnosis and the Immune Response." *International Journal of Psychosomatics,* 1985, 32(3), 34–36.

———. "Treating Dental Phobias through Past Life Therapy: A Case Report." *Journal of the Maryland State Dental Association,* 1984, 27(3), 137–139.

Head and V. Cranston. *Reincarnation: The Phoenix Fire Mysteries.* New York: Julian, 1977.

Hodson, G. *Reincarnation: Fact or Fallacy.* Wheaton, Illinois: The Theosophical Publishing House, 1967.

Korn, E. R. *Visualization: Use of Imagery in the Health Professions.* Homewood, Illinois: Dow Jones-Irwin, 1983.

Lazar, B. and C. Dempster. "Failures in Hypnosis and Hypnotherapy." *American Journal of Clinical Hypnosis.* 1982, 24(1), 48–54.

McKim, R. *Experiences in Visual Thinking*. Belmont, California: Wadsworth Publishing Co., 1972.

Mills, J. C., and R. J. Crowley. *Therapeutic Metaphors for the Child Within*. New York: Brunner/Mazel, Inc., 1986.

Newton, Michael. *Journey of Souls*. St. Paul: Llewellyn Publications, 1994.

Ostrander, S., and L. Schroeder. *Psychic Discoveries Behind the Iron Curtain*. New York: Bantam, 1970.

Richardson, A., and C. C. Taylor. "Vividness of Mental Imagery and Self-Induced Mood Change." *British Journal of Clinical Psychology*, 1982, 21, 111–117.

Richardson, A. *Mental Imagery*. New York: Springer Publishing Co., 1969, p. 8.

Rogo, D. S. *Exploring Psychic Phenomena*. Wheaton, Illinois: The Theosophical Publishing House, 1976.

Samuels, M., and N. Samuels. *Seeing with the Mind's Eye*. New York: Random House, Inc., 1975.

Sheikh, A., editor. *Anthology of Imagery Techniques*. Wisconsin: American Imagery Institute, 1986.

Sommer, R. *The Mind's Eye: Imagery in Everyday Life*. New York: Delacorte Press, 1978.

Targ, R., and K. Harary. *The Mind Race*. New York: Villard Books, 1984.

Tart, C. T. *Psi: Scientists Studies of the Psychic Realm*. New York: Dutton, 1977.

Wambach, H. *Life Before Life*. New York: Bantam, 1979.

Wester, W., and A. Smith. *Clinical Hypnosis*. New York: J. B. Lippincott, 1984.

Wolf, F. A. *Taking the Quantum Leap*. New York: Harper and Row, 1981.

———. *Parallel Universes: The Search for Other Worlds*. New York: Simon and Schuster, 1988.

Wolf, F. A., and B. Toben. *Space-Time and Beyond*. New York: Bantam Books, 1982.

INDEX

☾ LOOK FOR THE CRESCENT MOON

Llewellyn publishes hundreds of books on your favorite subjects! To get these exciting books, including the ones on the following pages, check your local bookstore or order them directly from Llewellyn.

ORDER BY PHONE

- Call toll-free within the U.S. and Canada, 1-800-THE MOON
- In Minnesota, call (612) 291-1970
- We accept VISA, MasterCard, and American Express

ORDER BY MAIL

- Send the full price of your order (MN residents add 7% sales tax) in U.S. funds, plus postage & handling to:

  Llewellyn Worldwide
  P.O. Box 64383, Dept. (K320–4)
  St. Paul, MN 55164–0383, U.S.A.

POSTAGE & HANDLING
(For the U.S., Canada, and Mexico)

- $4.00 for orders $15.00 and under
- $5.00 for orders over $15.00
- No charge for orders over $100.00

We ship UPS in the continental United States. We ship standard mail to P.O. boxes. Orders shipped to Alaska, Hawaii, The Virgin Islands, and Puerto Rico are sent first-class mail. Orders shipped to Canada and Mexico are sent surface mail.

International orders: Airmail—add freight equal to price of each book to the total price of order, plus $5.00 for each non-book item (audio tapes, etc.).

Surface mail—Add $1.00 per item.

Allow 4–6 weeks for delivery on all orders.
Postage and handling rates subject to change.

DISCOUNTS

We offer a 20% discount to group leaders or agents. You must order a minimum of 5 copies of the same book to get our special quantity price.

FREE CATALOG

Get a free copy of our color catalog, *New Worlds of Mind and Spirit*. Subscribe for just $10.00 in the United States and Canada ($30.00 overseas, airmail). Many bookstores carry *New Worlds*— ask for it!

VISIT OUR WEB SITE AT WWW.LLEWELLYN.COM FOR MORE INFORMATION.

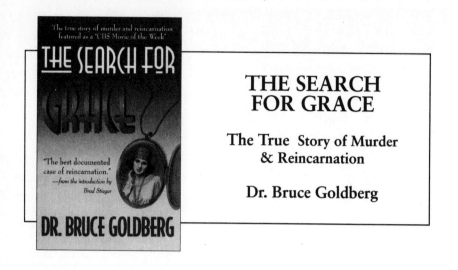

THE SEARCH FOR GRACE

The True Story of Murder & Reincarnation

Dr. Bruce Goldberg

The best documented case of reincarnation.
—from the introduction by Brad Steiger

An unsolved murder mystery on the books since 1927 ... one modern woman's obsession with an abusive lover ... and a karmic journey that winds through a maze of past lives—all of these unite into the *best*-documented case of reincarnation in the Western world.

The Search for Grace is the true story of Ivy, a 26-year-old pharmacist who sought the help of Dr. Bruce Goldberg to put a stop to her inexplainable attraction to John, her physically and psychologically abusive boyfriend. Under hypnosis, she discovered that John had been her lover—and her murderer—in 20 of her 46 past lives.

When Ivy recounts the details of her 46th life as roaring-twenties party girl Grace Doze, hypnotherapy and real-life dovetail into a dramatic twist of fate. It was May 19, 1927, when the body of Grace Doze turned up in a Buffalo, N.Y., creek. Her murder remained a mystery until 60 years later, when Dr. Goldberg put Ivy into a superconscious state, and Grace's true killer was brought to light for the world to see.

1-56718-318-2, 6 x 9, 288 pp., photos, softcover $12.95

LOOK YOUNGER, LIVE LONGER

Add 25 to 50 Years to Your Life, Naturally

Dr. Bruce Goldberg

Medical research has shown that your body's immune system is the most important factor in determining how quickly you will age. The key ingredient for keeping your immune system strong is a hormone produced by your own body called DHEA.

Now there's hope for everyone who desires to turn back time naturally, without the use of drugs or surgery. Scientific studies prove that meditative techniques, including self-hypnosis, can actually increase your body's production of DHEA, knocking years off your appearance and biological clock.

In *Look Younger, Live Longer* you will discover:

- How to use self-hypnosis to increase your body's *natural* production of DHEA to slow down the aging process
- How to look younger immediately
- Easy techniques to boost your brain power and improve memory
- An eating plan to reduce the cellular changes leading to old age symptoms and nutritional keys to halt aging skin *now*
- A step-by-step plan to reprogram the internal computer that may be aging you prematurely

Dr. Bruce Goldberg presents solid scientific and clinical evidence of how you can tap into the fountain of youth. Follow his recommendations and you will keep joy in your heart, a sparkle in your eyes and a spring in your step for many decades to come.

1-56718-321-2, 6 x 9, 224 pp. $12.95

SOUL HEALING

Dr. Bruce Goldberg

George: overcame lung cancer and a life of smoking through hypnotic programming.

Mary: tripled her immune system's response to AIDS with the help of age progression.

Now you, too, can learn to raise the vibrational rate of your soul (or subconscious mind) to stimulate your body's own natural healing processes. Explore several natural approaches to healing that include past life regression and future life progression, hypnotherapy, soulmates, angelic healing, near-death experiences, shamanic healing, acupuncture, meditation, yoga, and the new physics.

The miracle of healing comes from within. After reading *Soul Healing*, you will never view your life and the universe in the same way again.

1–56718–317–4, 304 pp., 6 x 9   **$14.95**